ORTHO'S All About

Building
Waterfalls,
Pools, and Streams

W9-BSE-052

Written by Charles M. Thomas and Richard M. Koogle

Meredith® Books
Des Moines, Iowa

Ortho® Books
An imprint of Meredith® Books

All About Building Waterfalls, Pools, and Streams
Editor: Marilyn Rogers
Project Editor: Kate Carter Frederick
Writers: Charles B. Thomas and Richard M. Koogle
Contributing Technical Consultant: James A. Lawrie
Contributing Technical Editor: Michael D. Smith
Senior Associate Design Director: Tom Wegner
Assistant Editor: Harijs Priekulis
Copy Chief: Terri Fredrickson
Editorial Operations Manager: Karen Schirm
Managers, Book Production: Pam Kvitne,
    Marjorie J. Schenkelberg
Contributing Copy Editor: Barbara Feller-Roth
Technical Proofreader: Fran Gardner
Contributing Proofreaders: Pegi Bevins, JoEllyn Witke
Contributing Illustrator: Mike Eagleton
Contributing Map Illustrator: Jana Fothergill
Contributing Prop/Photo Stylist: Carrie Hansen
Indexer: Donald Glassman
Electronic Production Coordinator: Paula Forest
Editorial and Design Assistant: Kathleen Stevens

**Additional Editorial Contributions from
    Art Rep Services**
Director: Chip Nadeau
Designer: lk Design
Illustrator: Rick Hanson

Meredith® Books
Editor in Chief: James D. Blume
Design Director: Matt Strelecki
Managing Editor: Gregory H. Kayko
Executive Editor, Gardening and Home Improvement:
    Benjamin W. Allen

Director, Sales, Special Markets: Rita McMullen
Director, Sales, Premiums: Michael A. Peterson
Director, Sales, Retail: Tom Wierzbicki
Director, Book Marketing: Brad Elmitt
Director, Operations: George A. Susral
Director, Production: Douglas M. Johnston

Meredith Publishing Group
President, Publishing Group: Stephen M. Lacy

Meredith Corporation
Chairman and Chief Executive Officer: William T. Kerr
Chairman of the Executive Committee: E.T. Meredith III

Thanks to
Beth Ann Edwards, Rosemary Kautzky, Mary Irene Swartz,
    Rick Osbourne, Aquascape Designs,

Photographers
    (Photographers credited may retain copyright ©
    to the listed photographs.)
L = Left, R = Right, C = Center, B = Bottom, T = Top
Aquascape Designs, Inc. : 10B, 19, 32, 33T, 42, 45TL,
    45TR, 48, 52B, 62, 72, 73R, 76, 79, 80, 81, 85, 88, 89
Andrew Drake/gardenIMAGE: 25B, 28
Jan Fetler: 26T, 70, 71
T. L. Gettings: 20B
Ed Gohlich: 49
Saxon Holt: 10, 11, 18, 40, 41, 46
Jerry Harpur: 61
Michael Landis: 39TR
James A. Lawrie: 33B, 65TL, 66
Lilypons Water Gardens: 21B, 36R, 43
Michael McKinley: 35
John A. Meeks: 14
Ortho Library: 37, 54, 86
Lark Smothermon/Woolly Bugger Studios: 13T, 21, 23, 25T,
    30, 31, 36L, 39BR, 44, 85
Steve Struse: 45B
Studio Central: 39CL, 39BL, 39C, 39CR
Tom Tracy: 55
Bill Uber/Van Ness Water Gardens: 16TR, 17B

Cover photo: Andrew Lawson. Garden design by Paul Dyer
    of the Very Interesting Landscape Co.

All of us at Ortho® Books are dedicated to providing you
with the information and ideas you need to enhance your
home and garden. We welcome your comments and
suggestions about this book. Write to us at:
    Meredith Corporation
    Ortho Gardening Books
    1716 Locust St.
    Des Moines, IA 50309–3023

If you would like to purchase any of our gardening, home
improvement, cooking, crafts, or home decorating and
design books, check wherever quality books are sold. Or visit
us at: meredithbooks.com

If you would like more information on other Ortho
products, call 800-225-2883 or visit us at: www.ortho.com

Note to the Readers: Due to differing conditions, tools,
and individual skills, Meredith Corporation assumes no
responsibility for any damages, injuries suffered, or losses
incurred as a result of following the information published
in this book. Before beginning any project, review the
instructions carefully, and if any doubts or questions remain,
consult local experts or authorities. Because codes and
regulations vary greatly, you always should check with
authorities to ensure that your project complies with all
applicable local codes and regulations. Always read and
observe all of the safety precautions provided by
manufacturers of any tools, equipment, or supplies,
and follow all accepted safety procedures.

Gently sloping terrain provides a natural location for a captivating waterfall. The water music created here attracts the attention of guests before they see the feature. If you don't have a naturally inclined site for a waterfall, build a berm with soil excavated when creating a pond.

Water invites the visitor to linger and absorb its tranquillity. A dock or a pebble beach enables people as well as wildlife to move to the water's edge and even wade into the pond.

WHY BUILD A WATER FEATURE?

As a life-giving and sustaining element, water is an essential part of any landscape. Moving or still, water in your landscape will entrance you and reward you with a variety of benefits. Water delights the beholder, whether it is peaceful and contemplative in a reflective pool or a quiet bog, or exciting in a rushing waterfall or stream.

A water feature that includes aquatic plants and fish captivates viewers with its fascinating rhythm of life and continual change. The magic of waterfalls applies no matter the climate, garden design, home architecture, or lifestyle.

A WATER FEATURE OFFERS SOMETHING FOR EVERYONE

■ An oasis of tranquillity to which you can retreat from the stress of everyday life.
■ The refreshing sound of moving water to wash away worries and calm the nerves.
■ The visual excitement of spilling, cascading, and rippling water.
■ The intriguing dance of nature among the plants, insects, birds, and other wildlife attracted to the water through the seasons.
■ The pleasure of watching darting ornamental fish and hearing the peaceful songs of frogs.
■ The magical presence of water running through the garden that draws you to sit outdoors to watch or putter.
■ A center of activity for viewing, sharing, and learning for people of all ages.

IT'S NOTHING NEW

The beauty of water features has generated a romantic and alluring mystique over millennia. Water features are popular because they transform an ordinary garden into a delightful retreat. Choose from a wealth of possibilities, from a small, simple container garden or a fountain to a still pool or a cascading stream.

Designing and building a water feature offer all sorts of appeal, whether you seek a creative outlet or a way to challenge your mechanical or building skills. Even if you don't view its design as an art form, a water feature becomes an artful addition to the landscape. Making a waterfall, a stream, or a pool offers new gardening opportunities as you decide which plants to include and whether or not to incorporate aquatic plants. Whatever your goals, completing the project—a permanent addition to your garden—will give you a sense of accomplishment.

In addition, a well-designed landscape that includes a carefully constructed water feature could increase your property's value by 10 to 12 percent, according to the Horticultural Research Institute. Depending on the design, you can use a water feature to resolve a landscape problem, such as a boring or sloping site, turning it into a decorative asset. Your design might help you build on top of soil that retains water or won't support much plant life other than weeds. Following a trend toward more environmentally friendly landscapes, the newest technology and concepts in constructing water features imitate nature and give you ways to transform your property into a beautiful oasis.

WHY HESITATE?

Despite all the compelling reasons to make a beautiful water feature, many people hesitate. Construction often intimidates people and may prevent them from diving into a project. That's where this book comes in. Use this guide to simplify the process as we lead you through it step-by-step. Begin by considering your options for building materials and equipment; then proceed to design and build your dream of a water feature.

Just set your sights on making the most natural-looking pond, stream, bog, or waterfall. Then prepare yourself for the delights and satisfaction it will provide for years to come.

TYPES OF WATER FEATURES

Landscaping with water presents a wealth of design opportunities as well as a challenge to the imagination. Because water is part of the natural world, it easily harmonizes with any landscape, any regional climate, and any architectural style. In dry areas, a water feature is a welcome oasis; in cold regions, it brings year-round interest.

Water attracts people as well as wildlife. It brings us closer to nature, or even to cherished memories. Recall your grandmother's lily pond or the waterfall, stream, lake, or pond that inspired you on a trip or a visit to a public garden. You can capture these memories with your own feature. Choose one that has meaning for you and fits your lifestyle.

Building a water garden in the middle of a deck is not all that daunting. When you're through, you'll have a small feature within steps of the house as well as a comfortable place to enjoy it.

CHOOSING A POND

Almost any watertight container qualifies for this simple feature. For example, transform a half whiskey barrel into an attractive container pond for a small patio. Add a bamboo spout for the soothing music of a trickling fountain. Even a 12-inch bowl can be a garden with aquatic plants such as umbrella palm, dwarf papyrus, or duckweed,

bringing life to confined places, from a patio or deck to a balcony or courtyard.

Perhaps you prefer a naturalistic, irregular water lily pond. Informal ponds are a favorite feature in American landscaping. An array of other aquatic plants may also inhabit the pond. Fish darting among lily pads add exciting motion to the scene, and hard-working snails provide a study in slow motion.

Formal pools—rectangles, circles, and ovals—appear frequently in parks and estate and public gardens. They enhance home landscapes as well, suiting small areas such as townhouse gardens or nooks in a quiet outdoor room. Their symmetry appeals to our sense of order and regularity, and the solid building materials typically used to make a formal pool suggest strength and permanence.

Water features help naturalize a deck by softening its hard edges. Combine a small pond with potted plants to transform a barren expanse of decking into a garden area. Use these elements on the deck surface or at ground level, extending under and around the deck edge to integrate into the landscape.

GO FISH

Although koi and other fish have special requirements outside the scope of this book, goldfish thrive in water gardens. They benefit from the freshly oxygenated water of a waterfall, especially during hot, muggy summer weather.

A passion for bird watching or a love of nature prompts many people to construct a water feature as part of a wildlife habitat.

Well-placed stepping-stones lead the eye of the observer through a water garden. They provide closeup viewing and convenient positions for pond maintenance.

Water attracts wildlife such as butterflies, dragonflies, birds, turtles, and other creatures, depending on where you live. By creating a water environment, you'll reap the benefits of any natural place, its beauty and peace.

WATERFALLS AND STREAMS

Waterfalls and streams contribute motion and sound to a landscape. The design of a watercourse determines the emotions it elicits—exciting or calming, energizing or restful. Streams and waterfalls, regardless of their size, add variety to the landscape. What's more, a waterfall or stream may provide a solution for areas otherwise difficult to landscape, such as steep slopes, rocky terrain, or deep shade. A forceful waterfall helps minimize traffic noise. Whichever water feature you choose will set your landscape apart from the ordinary.

BOG GARDENS

Constructing a bog garden puts you on the cutting edge of landscape and garden designs. Bog gardens not only mimic a swampy, natural habitat, but they also present an opportunity to turn a poorly draining, soggy area into a beautiful garden teeming with wildlife. For plant lovers, bogs display a vast array of seldom-seen native plants that thrive in wet or moist soil. Known as marginal plants, most grow best with wet roots, but some adapt to periodically dry conditions. All offer another opportunity to explore a vast plant palette.

Bogs can be part of a pond or a separate aquatic feature. When incorporated into the edge of a pond with fish, bogs act as a filter, providing an ideal mechanism for enhancing the quality of the water. Fish waste-polluted water recirculating through the bog carries nutrients to plants and beneficial bacteria growing there. They in turn clean the water and enhance the quality of life in the fishpond. Without filtering, fish die from the toxicity of their own waste.

THE BEAUTY OF CHOICES

Choosing a water feature is like choosing a home: The choice has to suit who you are, how you spend your time, and what you expect from your surroundings. A powerful waterfall gives self-expression and fulfillment to some. For others, nothing is finer than a quiet waterfall with a stream flowing to a bog garden and lily pond. Still others enjoy growing aquatic plants in a deck or patio water garden. The beauty is that the choice is yours.

One of the main attractions of water gardens is the opportunity to choose and grow a wide variety of aquatic plants in addition to terrestrial plants that prefer moist or wet soil.

A raised or partially raised pond provides a solution for building on a rocky site or where the groundwater level is high.

WHAT'S NEW?

A revolutionary approach to water gardening employs beneficial bacteria to colonize gravel beds and biological filters and results in crystal clear water. Combined with plants, fish, and scavengers along with required equipment, the balance of elements imitates nature in managing water quality. A traditional balanced approach uses a particular proportion of plants, fish, beneficial bacteria, and scavengers to maintain water quality. The fish population is limited, but optional pumps and filters may be used to support additional fish. For more details turn to page 18.

If your new landscape calls for a large water feature, such as a pond, stream, or waterfall, you'll want to excavate before you install a lawn and plant trees. If you plan to tuck a formal concrete feature into an existing small courtyard, consider using concrete blocks instead of poured concrete where it's impossible for a ready-mix truck to reach the site.

Concrete block water features work best in frost-free regions where there is no danger of earth movement. Use a flexible pond liner to prevent water loss if the pond cracks.

BUILDING MATERIALS

Choosing the most appropriate building materials for constructing a pool, waterfall, or stream will have a major impact on your satisfaction with the finished project. Select the basic materials, including liners and edging, depending on the style, design, and size of your feature as well as your preferences and budget. Each building material has pros and cons. For example, consider the ease or difficulty of installation and how long the material is likely to last. The materials and construction methods you choose will also depend on the site and your region's climate.

Include a strategy in your plan for incorporating the water feature into your site. If you live in a cold climate, consider how freezing and thawing affect some materials. In any region, ultraviolet light (UV rays from the sun) causes plastic liner materials to become brittle and crack over time.

The selection of gravel, rock, and boulders also depends on where you live and the variety of indigenous materials available. Rocks from a local quarry will appear more natural than imported materials. You'll need flat rocks when building a spillway for a waterfall. Embellish a spillway and the edging of other features with a different shape and size of rock for a natural look.

Check with local and state authorities for permits that may be required before you begin any construction project. Ask local utilities to mark underground cables or pipes before you start digging.

LINERS

A liner is required to make your water feature watertight. Options include flexible or preformed liners, or a base of concrete or clay. You'll find preformed liners made of fiberglass or plastic in a variety of shapes and sizes. Compare the types of liners and imagine yourself installing them.

Consider using an additional sub-liner or underlayment as a protective layer between the liner and the soil. Many kinds of flexible and preformed liners as well as underlayments are readily available from aquatic garden suppliers, building supply stores, and mail-order sources.

CONCRETE AND CLAY

If properly constructed, concrete pools last for decades. However, concrete construction is more difficult and costly than the alternatives. Building a concrete pond may require hiring professionals who have the necessary expertise and tools. Ideally, concrete should be embedded with heavy-duty steel wire mesh or reinforcing rods (rebar) for stability and durability. Gunite, concrete sprayed on steel reinforcing, efficiently forms a naturalistic pond. Concrete blocks or a combination of concrete and stone, bricks, or decorative tile offer additional building options, particularly for aboveground water features.

Mortar, a form of concrete, is used for building with block or brick and making seals between them as well as for embedding stone, brick, or comparable edging materials. Mortar tends to separate after repeated freezing and thawing. Alternatively, you may use black urethane foam. It forms a lasting seal that helps prevent leaking because it expands when applied and won't deteriorate over time.

Compacted clay-bottom ponds hold water naturally. They are constructed on land with clay-based soil or built with clay that's brought to the site. Their water-holding capacity is sometimes enhanced by adding bentonite, a powdered clay made from volcanic ash.

EDGING

Edging materials include rocks, cut stone, bricks, pavers, decorative tile, concrete, wood decking, turf, and plants. All give a finished look to the edge of a water feature. Not only does edging conceal the liner, but it also helps define the style of your water feature, integrating it with the surrounding landscape and architectural elements. Choose edging materials accordingly.

FLEXIBLE LINERS AND UNDERLAYMENT

Use a spirit level resting on a long, straight board to check that the edge of the pool is level along its entire perimeter. If one edge is higher than another, add and tamp soil until the sides are even.

Line a stream excavation with a flexible liner on a warm, sunny day. A PVC liner is more flexible and easier to work with when it is warm.

The overwhelming favorite choice of material for a water feature, flexible liners offer unrivaled potential for design creativity, simple installation, reasonable cost, dependable longevity, easy repair, and low maintenance.

Whatever shape you design and excavate for a water feature, a flexible liner conforms to it. A compact shape makes installation easier and less expensive. A complex design with lots of thin fingers wastes liner material. It increases the amount of tucking and folding of the liner, making installation more difficult.

Installing a flexible liner calls for a protective underlayment, typically a layer of geotextile material or carpet, which goes in the pond excavation before installing the flexible liner or preformed unit. It serves as a barrier to prevent stones or other objects in the ground from damaging the liner or shell.

COMPARING LINERS

Flexible liners survive easily in most climates. After years of exposure to UV light from the sun and extremely cold weather, however, they become brittle and then crack and leak. Polyethylene and polyvinyl chloride (PVC) liners are more prone to brittleness than liners made of ethylene propylene diene monomer (EPDM), butyl rubber, and PVC-E (E for enhanced). Other threats to flexible liners are sharp or pointed objects, which can cause punctures. The toughest flexible liner, Xavan (a patented product), resists punctures and tears.

In areas where earth tremors occur, flexible liners don't crack as do preformed liners or concrete. If a leak occurs in a flexible liner, it's relatively easy to repair.

To make a flexible liner last longer, design a water feature to prevent the liner's exposure to UV light. Water alone won't do the job. Its level fluctuates due to evaporation, thereby exposing the liner to the sun and its drying effects. What's more, UV rays penetrate clear water. Cover any exposed liner edge with soil, rocks, or plants to protect it and to give your water feature a finished look. Edging should adequately shield any liner showing above the water's surface.

POLYETHYLENE LINER

This lightweight, inexpensive option typically lasts only one season. Polyethylene readily takes its intended shape, but it lacks the sturdiness required of a pond liner. Use it to line a container garden that leaks or a half whiskey barrel that still smells of its former contents. Polyethylene is also useful as a bog garden liner in frost-free climates.

PVC AND PVC-E LINERS

PVC and PVC-E liners generally last beyond their 10- or 12-year guarantee. Use the standard 20-mil thickness (a mil equals .001 inch) for water features. Both types cost about the same; they're the least expensive liners that last 10 years or more. They cost about 25 percent less than rubber, yet resist tears and punctures better than rubber (PVC-E is more supple, making it easier to install).

EPDM AND RUBBER LINERS

EPDM and butyl rubber liners often last beyond their typical guarantee of 20 years. Geography largely determines their availability. In North America, for example, you'll most likely find EPDM; in Europe, you'll find butyl. Their 45-mil thickness, the industry standard, makes them heavier than PVC (an installation disadvantage) but more flexible than PVC (an installation advantage). Make certain that the liner is

fish-safe; check the package label or ask the dealer from whom you purchase it. Similar liners made for swimming pools, for instance, are impregnated with anti-algae material, which is toxic to fish. However, old swimming pool liners that have lost their anti-algae effectiveness pose no danger. EPDM designed for roofing may also be harmful to fish.

Lay a cushion of sand on the bottom of the excavation to smooth out the area and help protect the liner from punctures. Center the liner over the excavation, then begin to smooth it out.

HOW TO DETERMINE THE LINER SIZE

Purchase a flexible liner by the square foot. Determine the size of your water feature before you purchase a liner for it.

Here's how:

Imagine your pond as a rectangle, even though it may be round or irregular. Make sure the rectangle includes the farthest points of the pond. Then consider how deep the pond will be. The liner size equals the length (l) plus two times the depth (d), plus 2 feet, multiplied by the width (w) plus two times the depth (d), plus 2 feet. This allows a 1-foot margin all the way around the perimeter. Professionals often add only 6 inches around the perimeter, leaving little margin for error. You

decide how much risk you're willing to take.

A pond whose imaginary rectangle measures 15 feet by 10 feet and is 1½ feet deep needs a liner 20 feet (15 + 1½ + 1½ + 2 = 20) by 15 feet (10 + 1½ + 1½ + 2 = 15); 20×15 = a 300-square-foot liner. Make any number of depth and surface configurations, including shelves, with a given-size liner; the same formula applies.

At this point, don't worry about figuring the volume (number of gallons) your water feature will hold. Some suppliers give the maximum gallons possible using their liner (or other product) and assuming a given depth. You will need the volume in

order to determine the fish-carrying capacity and to figure the appropriate size of optional features such as a waterfall, pump, mechanical filter, UV clarifier, and water treatments.

Figure the volume of a pond or other feature by calculating how many cubic feet are in it, then multiplying the number of cubic feet by 7.5 (because each cubic foot contains 7.5 gallons of water).

To size a liner for a finished excavation, measure the length and width of the excavation using a flexible tape. Add 2 feet to each measurement. Unpack a liner only when you're certain it's the right size.

FLEXIBLE LINERS AND UNDERLAYMENT
continued

OTHER OPTIONS

Xavan, a nonwoven polypropylene material that is spun and heat-bonded for added durability, resists tearing and puncturing. Xavan costs more but lasts longer than other materials because it is more resistant to ultraviolet light. At 22 mil it weighs one-third less than a standard rubber liner, making it easier to lift and adjust during installation. Its supple and malleable nature makes it easier to manage during installation than PVC or rubber.

COMPARING FLEXIBLE LINERS

Material	Thickness	Typical life span
Polyethylene	10 mil	1 year
PVC	20 mil	10 years
PVC-E	20 mil	15 years
Xavan	22 mil	25 years
EPDM	45 mil	20 years
Butyl	45 mil	20 years

FOUNDATION UNDER A BOULDER

Large boulders at the edge of a pond (or in the midst of it) require a concrete support along with extra layers of liner and under-layment to prevent leaks.

Boulder

Layers of flexible liner

Underlayment

3/8- to 1/2-inch steel rebar

4- to 6-inch-thick concrete pad

The black color of flexible liners sometimes confuses first-time pond builders. Once the liner is installed, however, viewers see the water, plants, and fish—not the black liner. It makes the water mirrorlike, as in a Monet masterpiece, reflecting sky, trees, and nearby shrubbery. Moreover, the blackness makes the water seem deeper, even mysterious. Liners come in other colors, including gray and dark green (a color similar to beneficial mosslike algae that forms naturally). Avoid blue and aquamarine liners, which proclaim their artificialness.

UNDERLAYMENT

The underlayment, an additional clothlike layer between the soil and the liner, protects the liner from exterior damage. Use it to cover both the bottom and outside walls of the area excavated for your water feature, because the subtle movement that occurs over time subjects the liner to potential damage. The heavy weight of water pushing the liner against rock, stones, or any other sharp-edged object might cause leaks. Underlayment reduces this possibility. Commercial underlayment is manufactured for landscape use and is designed to survive for decades in the ground.

Used carpeting and rugs qualify as alternative and effective underlayment materials. Even staple-free cardboard and old newspapers offer liner protection. They decay eventually, but not rapidly, because they're not exposed to air and light.

Before installing the underlayment, place a 1- to 2-inch layer of sand on the bottom of the excavation. This helps to give the pond a smooth bottom as well as a good foundation underfoot. Avoid using sand on the sides; it tends to shift downward over time, leaving sides without cushioning. This step is not needed if your soil is sandy, free of stones and tree roots, and poses no threat to the underlayment or liner.

BOULDER ISLANDS

If you wish to create the striking effect of one or more immense boulders rising from the pond, take precautions to avoid a disaster. Instead of installing a liner around an island of rocks or soil, build the island after installing the pond liner.

The heavy weight of large boulders requires a 4- to 6-inch-deep reinforced-concrete foundation beneath the underlayment to prevent damage to the liner. When planning a design that includes large boulders, use a lumber frame to form the concrete slab.

PREFORMED LINERS

Rigid, preformed liners for pools, streams, and waterfalls offer the easiest and fastest means of constructing a water feature. When properly installed, they will be leak-free. Rigid liners are also puncture-resistant and easy to clean. The best preformed units are made of ¼-inch fiberglass and last 50 years or more; high-density polyethylene units last at least 20 years. Their quality and longevity justify the higher cost compared to flexible liners. Although rigid, these liners flex enough to prevent cracking when their contents freeze during winter. Their sloping sides cause ice to lift slightly as it forms and expands.

Some preformed units are designed as modules that link together to create a free-form effect. With sufficient space and a gentle slope to the terrain, you could combine a pool, a stream, a waterfall, and an additional basin in a pleasing configuration. You may decide to purchase a filter unit that doubles as a waterfall. Its proper installation entails bolting the forms together and sealing them with marine silicone.

SIZE, SHAPE, AND COLOR

Preformed liners for ponds, streams, or waterfalls come in a variety of shapes, sizes, and colors. Preformed units suit small and formal designs, especially in natural or geometric shapes. If you don't find units in the shape you want, check with other suppliers. The shape and configuration of forms vary among manufacturers. You'll find units as large as 12 feet wide, 20 feet long, and 2 feet deep; others are smaller and too shallow (less than 15 inches) to be practical as fish ponds. Many designs include plant shelves; choose a liner with shelves no less than 9 inches wide.

Don't worry about figuring the number of gallons a preformed unit holds. The manufacturer will list volume with the product's specifications. Most units simulate stone colors, such as gray, brown, and black; select a color similar to the native rock you will use to edge the water feature. This will help integrate your pool, stream, or waterfall into the landscape and give it a more natural look.

Blending rigid forms into the landscape takes extra care because the edges can be more difficult to disguise than those of flexible liners. Nevertheless, with the skilled placement of plants, along with native rock, brick, tile, and wood edging, you can achieve the desired results. If a preformed pool will sit above ground or partially above ground, plan on building a facade of some sort around it to hide the liner.

PREPARATION PROVES WISE

Careful site preparation and liner setup determine whether preformed units function optimally. Basically, you will dig a hole in the ground the size and shape of your preformed unit, lower the liner in place, and backfill around it with soil. Sand provides a stable base of support because it compacts readily and proves easy to rework if you must make adjustments to the excavation. Purchase enough sand to lay a 2-inch-deep bed under your preformed liner. Preformed constructions must be level in order to look right and prevent the liner from buckling or warping when filled with water.

Unless you already are sure where you want to install your water feature, the mobility of preformed units gives them another advantage. After acquiring your preformed units, move them around until you're completely satisfied with their location; then begin excavating. Once installed, if the original site of your water feature proves less than pleasing, you may relocate it.

Prefabricated, high-density polyethylene units enable you to make endless configurations for your water feature. Link two pools via a cascading streamlet (center) or a simple spillway (bottom right).

After skillful edging with bricks and concrete pavers, complete a pond's surroundings with a variety of plants.

CONCRETE PONDS

Most ponds were made of concrete until the1960s when new, flexible liners presented a less costly, easier-to-install option. Poured concrete and concrete block are classic-looking building materials that can last decades. Conversely, concrete's high cost and challenging construction make it daunting for an inexperienced builder. If improperly installed, a concrete pool will crack, leak, and cause infinite frustrations. Avoid using concrete to line a stream. It's expensive and doesn't look natural.

If you prefer, combine the beauty and durability of concrete with a flexible or preformed liner. The liner eliminates the need to neutralize the concrete before adding plants or fish, and if the concrete cracks, it won't leak. Also consider finishing a concrete-lined pond with a handsome exterior framework of brick, treated wood, or tile. Capping concrete walls with brick, stone, or pavers gives a pond a stylish look as well.

POURED CONCRETE OR BLOCKS

A poured-concrete structure requires preparing an excavation and wood forms to shape the walls and hold the concrete while it sets. The base and sides of the excavation should be firmly tamped. Cover the level base with a 4- to 6-inch layer of gravel to help prevent cracking. Sandwich wire mesh or metal rods in between two layers of poured concrete to provide reinforcement and strength. Alternatively, have a professional spray the wire-reinforced form with layers of concrete, known as gunite or shotcrete. Paint

Using concrete block to construct a formal pool offers an alternative building method. A level excavation and properly laid concrete blocks help ensure that your pond has straight sides and a level top.

For added strength, reinforcing rods will be inserted into the hollow concrete blocks before being filled with concrete. Renting a soil tamper makes it easy to smooth the excavation. The low end will house water lilies.

Once a flexible pond liner is installed, decorative stone caps the concrete block and hides the liner from view. Secured with mortar, the stones create a solid edge that's strong enough for sitting.

This concrete-block pool, waterproofed with a flexible liner, successfully survives freezing winters. Use concrete blocks to create a geometric shape for your formal pool.

the inside of a concrete pool with a waterproof sealant for water gardens if you like.

Concrete blocks offer a simpler way to construct a pond. Stacked hollow blocks, reinforced with metal rods and filled with concrete, make a formidable structure. Build shelves for plants by shaping the excavation to support them or stack additional blocks along the pond wall to form shelves. Line the pond with a flexible or preformed liner. Top the edges with mortared block, brick, or stone.

In regions with cold winters and freezing-thawing cycles, the sides of a concrete pool should slope outward by about 20 degrees overall to allow water in the pool to freeze and expand without cracking the concrete.

BRICK OR WOODEN-WALL PONDS

Construct a raised- or partially raised-wall pond by making a concrete-lined excavation and aboveground walls of brick or wood. Building such a pond completely on top of the ground would spell a collapse, but this method entails less excavating up front and easier maintenance in the long run. Brick provides a neat, rustic look; wood appears informal and natural in many settings.

Use engineering-quality solid bricks for best results. Purchase a flexible or preformed liner for your pond, if you wish; just be careful to conceal the liner edge with a cap of brick or stonework. Landscape timbers or railroad ties, drilled and reinforced with metal rods, form a decorative aboveground exterior frame.

IN COLD CLIMATES

To ensure its success, build a poured-concrete pond as you would a swimming pool. The walls and base must be at least 6 inches thick. Pour or spray concrete all at once (with no seams) over steel reinforcement until you achieve the required thickness.

HOW MUCH CONCRETE?

If you want to order enough concrete ready-mix (delivered by a contractor) to make 6-inch-thick walls that withstand a cold climate, use this formula. First, measure the outside dimensions (width × height) of each wall and the pond's bottom; then add the five numbers to determine the total area in square feet. Multiply the total by the thickness of the concrete (6 inches = 0.5 feet) to determine the number of cubic feet. Divide this number by 27 to conclude how many cubic yards of concrete to order. Estimate for a curved or irregular-shape pond by using an imaginary rectangle to figure the area and adding a 10 percent margin of error.

REINFORCED CONCRETE PERIMETER COLLAR

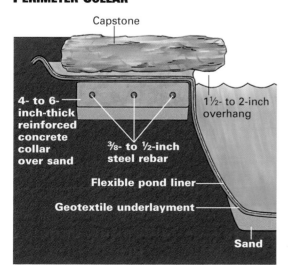

A concrete collar supports the rock edging around a pond and reinforces the edge's stability.

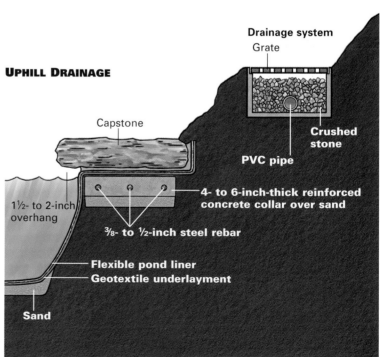

When building a water feature into the side of a slope, install a drainage system uphill from it to divert runoff from the pond. A catch basin, as here, is aesthetic and moves water efficiently.

EDGING

Stacked rocks of various sizes disguise the edge of a liner and create a realistic look for a water feature. Flat rocks, adequately secured, provide places to stand or step across.

Grass or other plants soften the effect of rock edging around water features. The same principal applies to formal ponds as well as to natural-looking features.

Edging materials add the finishing touch to a pond, stream, or waterfall. Enhance the aesthetic appeal of a natural-looking feature by concealing the exposed edges of the liner. Use edging to protect the liner from the harsh effects of the sun. A slightly raised edge also protects the pond from water runoff from the surrounding landscape.

Consider the look and function of your water feature when choosing edging material. Formal pond designs usually have geometric shapes, a level capstone, and one type of edging; informal ponds are often irregular in shape and include more than one type of edging. Edging gives birds and other wildlife access to your pond or stream. Even if you don't anticipate people standing near the water, construct the edging with safety in mind. Ensure the edging can withstand your weight combined with that of a visitor or two.

Edging a preformed water feature is more difficult than concealing a flexible liner. Unless the surrounding area is paved, take extra steps to disguise the rim. If you use heavy rocks or pavers as edging, support them with a foundation of concrete blocks or a layer of crushed stone topped with sand buried around the perimeter of the liner to hold up the lip. Make sure that the edging stones overhang the edge by 2 inches, or enough to conceal it.

NATURAL-LOOKING PONDS AND STREAMS

A concrete edge along a stream doesn't look natural. Instead, consider hiding the liner

edge under a ledge of soil topped with a combination of rocks and plants for the most natural look. Placing large, flat-topped rocks at strategic points along the stream provides steps as well as seating. A grouping of various-size rocks looks natural. If you have a large pond with a flexible liner, try creating a gently sloping pebble beach along one side, which allows wildlife to wade and bathe or wash their food in the shallow water.

ROCK AND STONE: These popular edging materials provide a look that's as natural as the ponds and streams they border. Choose rocks indigenous to your area; if there are no rocks in the native landscape, buy rocks that blend naturally with the local terrain. Granite and slate are hard and long-lasting. Their strata, or layers, when exposed, add a rugged beauty to the water's edge. They're well-suited to waterfalls because running water won't wear away the stone. Sedimentary rocks, including sandstone and limestone, are readily available and reasonably priced edging materials. However, these soft rocks deteriorate over time.

Avoid rocks that present a hazard to pond inhabitants. Fresh-cut limestone can make the water toxic to fish, and rainwater leaches the toxins into the pond even when the rocks are set beyond the water level. Stabilize rocks or stones with mortar and reinforcing materials so that overhanging rocks are less likely to fall into the water or shift under the weight of a visitor. One or more large boulders at the pond's edge create a dramatic effect, but plan for extra concrete reinforcement to support the weight of the boulders. To create a visual transition, surround boulders with smaller rocks of the same type. Also consider placing some stones partly submerged in the water.

PLANTS: Create a naturally soft, pleasing look by alternating plants between areas of rocks; avoid encircling the water feature with a necklace of rocks. Low-growing evergreens work well along the perimeter of most water features. Add plants after completing pond construction and installing edging.

TURF: Grass growing to the edge of the water feature looks neat and natural. It provides a good surface to reach the water to do maintenance or to observe fish. Skim grass clippings out of the water after mowing. Algae growth results as the high nitrogen in grass disturbs the ecological balance of the pond. Avoid using lawn chemicals, such as herbicides and fertilizers, that might run into your pond or stream when it rains and wreak havoc with the pond life.

FORMAL PONDS

Cut stone, decorative tiles, cast concrete pieces, or bricks typically edge formal water gardens. Arrange them in the geometric pattern of your choice; combine two or more types for an unusual, decorative look. Experiment by combining stones and colors at the water's edge to make sure you will be happy with the results. If your pond has curved edges, consider using retaining-wall blocks with a trapezoidal shape.

Set edging on a concrete collar or a 3-inch-deep bed of leveled crushed stone; use mortar to hold the stone, tile, or block in place. Bricks and some sedimentary rocks could raise the pH level of the water and possibly harm fish. Test the water regularly and adjust the pH level accordingly.

WOOD EDGING AND DECKING

Wood looks handsome when combined with turf and other edging materials or as the surface for a deck or walkway. However, do not use treated lumber. It can leach chemicals into a water feature and pose a toxic threat to plants and fish. Use rot-resistant woods, such as cedar or redwood, or manufactured composite woods. If you select redwood, let it age for a year until it turns gray. Fresh redwood contains toxic tannins.

If you like the look of wood edging, consider setting treated timbers, cut pier-style and stood upright, in a bed of concrete around the perimeter of the pool. Alternatively, build a deck over the edge of the water or along the perimeter of the water feature. An overhanging deck offers a place to sit, feed fish, or just watch the water.

A stone patio in a desert climate becomes a welcoming oasis with the addition of a shallow pond. River rocks and simple plantings naturalize the scene.

The combination of brick edging, a compact pond, and a small fountain makes this an ideal water feature for a confined urban site.

Decorative tiles reflect personal style. Select tiles that complement your home and garden.

A properly stocked and balanced water garden requires little added mechanical equipment. Ideally, you will need to spend a few minutes each week keeping your pond in good health.

BALANCED AND REVOLUTIONARY APPROACHES TO BUILDING AND STOCKING A WATER FEATURE

BALANCED APPROACH

PLANTS: Cover up to 75 percent of the water surface area with floating plants: 1 bunch of submerged plants per 1 to 2 square feet of surface area; marginal plants as desired.

SCAVENGERS: 1 black Japanese snail per 1 to 2 square feet of surface area.

FISH: 1 inch of goldfish (6-inch maximum length per fish) per 5 to 10 gallons of water. Koi require double the amount of water allotted for goldfish.

EQUIPMENT: None required; optional biological filter, UV clarifier, and pumps.

REVOLUTIONARY APPROACH

PLANTS, SCAVENGERS, FISH, AND BACTERIA: In balance as in nature. Limit fish to 1 inch of fish per square foot of water.

STONE AND ROCK: Divide square footage of pond surface area by 65 = number of tons of stone (granite) rounded up to nearest half ton; tons of stone × .45 = number of tons of gravel (washed) rounded up to the nearest half ton to cover bottom of pond.

EQUIPMENT: Biological filter, skimmer, and recirculating pump.

EQUIPMENT

Think of your water feature as an ecological system. Stocked with assorted aquatic plants, fish, and scavengers, it becomes a balanced system that largely takes care of itself. Not only does the aquatic life, including plants and creatures, add incomparable beauty and interest to a water feature, but it also earns its keep, so to speak, by working to control algae and benefit water quality.

Some people choose minimal equipment to enhance nature's efforts in maintaining the water feature's biological balance. Others invest in sophisticated filtration systems in order to achieve pristine water (and an absence of the algae that turns water green).

One way or another, your ability to control the water quality hinges on your understanding of the interdependence of plant and animal life and the bacteria that are necessary to life's balances. Your approach in designing and constructing the water feature, as well as to maintaining water quality, determines how you will equip and stock the water feature.

TWO APPROACHES TO ALGAE

Two construction approaches address the issue of controlling algae in a water feature. With the first, the balanced approach, a key component are the aquatic plantings, which absorb nutrients that otherwise stimulate algae growth. Scavengers and a limited fish population helps manage fish waste, which encourages algae. Beneficial bacteria colonize the pond sides and bottom. A recirculating pump and other equipment may be part of the system—or not. A properly balanced pond can thrive for years without cleaning.

The clear-water approach emphasizes a balance among plants, fish, rocks, and beneficial bacteria. With this approach, a layer of stones and gravel on the bottom of the water feature harbors beneficial bacteria, which transform toxic ammonia (from fish waste) to relatively benign nitrate. A pump, filter, and skimmer are standard components for this approach. The result is crystal-clear water. Waterfalls and streams may be added to oxygenate the water, enhancing its quality. A pond built with the clear-water approach needs an annual power wash to remove debris that accumulates in the gravel.

MANAGING WATER QUALITY

Understanding the nitrogen cycle (the relationship among nutrients in the water, fish, fish food, fish waste, beneficial pond bacteria, plant absorption of nitrate, and green pond water) gives you a fuller appreciation of your water feature as well as the importance of nature in managing water quality.

Mechanical filters help keep water clear by trapping particles or debris that cloud water. Biological filters, or biofilters, go a step further by helping to detoxify water. They use beneficial bacteria as part of the nitrogen cycle, breaking down ammonia (toxic) to nitrite (toxic) to nitrate (promotes algae growth). Plant filters carry the nitrogen cycle further by removing nitrate from the water. Skimmers remove floating debris before it contaminates the pond. Submersible or surface pumps force water into pipes or tubes, thereby powering filters, fountains, waterfalls, and streams. The mechanical requirements will determine the choice of a pump.

Finding equipment for building a water feature has become easier than ever. Compare quality and prices when you shop at nurseries, garden centers, home improvement stores, and mail-order sources that offer water-gardening materials.

Manufacturers make it easy for water gardeners to match the most appropriate equipment to the design of their water feature. A pond kit makes it even easier.

AQUATIC LIFE

Exotic koi need a roomy pond, at least 18 to 24 inches deep, where they can swim, find shade, and hide.

The decisions you make about adding aquatic plants and fish to your water feature influence not only its design but also how it functions and your choice of additional equipment. If you plan to build a fishpond, for example, you'll make it deeper than a garden pond. If you stock your fishpond with koi or other fish, incorporate a biological filter into your recirculation system.

The black Japanese snail doesn't eat plants; it cleans up algae, decaying vegetation, and wasted fish food.

In a sense, plants and fish function as equipment in a water feature. Aquatic plants, desirable kinds of algae, and fish live in harmony when a pond reaches a natural balance, without using equipment. Knowing the natural ratios of aquatic life help you stock a pond appropriately. A balance of plants, fish, and other scavengers contributes to algae control and water quality.

Both plant and animal life benefit from sharing the same habitat. Plants provide shade, shelter, and food for fish, while fish waste provides nutrients for plants. Plants also compete with algae for nutrients and sunlight. The larger your water feature, the more plants you'll probably want to include in your design, as long as they cover no more than 65 to 75 percent of the water's surface. When foliage covers much of the water's surface, it blocks sunlight, thus reducing algae growth. Submerged plants help keep the pond water clear. Marginal plants blend the water feature with the landscape. Floating plants also absorb nutrients and deter algae by blocking light. The variety of plants you choose is important in terms of how they function. Additionally, the combination of textures, colors, and fragrances adds beauty and seasonal interest to the water feature.

Water lilies enjoy widespread popularity among water gardeners for their serene beauty and reliable habits. The family *Nymphaea* is typically divided into two groups: tropical and hardy water lilies. Include all kinds of water lilies in your water feature to enjoy their blooms both day and night, from spring through fall. They bloom most reliably in calm water.

Fish contribute to the balance by eating overexuberant plants as well as algae if they're not overfed with commercial food. In addition, fish eat mosquitoes and other insects. Scavengers, such as snails, graze on algae and decaying matter, contributing to the ecological balance.

One way or the other, if your water feature includes fish, their waste must be detoxified with bacteria and plants or equipment in order for the fish to be healthy and survive. Aeration, in the form of a waterfall or fountain, adds oxygen to the water and allows you to add more fish than the pond otherwise would support. A water feature will also attract creatures of various kinds: birds, frogs, dragonflies, and others.

With or without added equipment, a simple pool or stream becomes a captivating water garden with the added dimension of fish and plants. Aquatic life should enhance the feature, not dominate the setting. The water itself should remain the focus of a water feature.

PUMPS

The splashing music of water as it moves and recirculates adds to the appeal of a water feature. It takes the right size pump to move water from a pool through tubing or pipes and other equipment to a waterfall, fountain, or stream. Just as you need to know how you plan to use a pump in order to choose the right type and size for the job, you must also identify how water will flow and how much resistance it will meet along the way.

Ease the selection by asking yourself these questions:

■ What kind of water feature do you envision? (How will you use the pump? How many gph—gallons per hour—will it require?)

■ What size is the feature? (How much water will flow through the pump? How many gph are needed to operate the feature?)

■ What else will the pump do? (Will it recirculate water through a filter, over a waterfall, or in a stream?)

■ For features where water returns downhill to the pond, how high above the water surface is the point where water discharges in a waterfall? What is the width of water flowing over the spillway? How thick a sheet of water do you want going over the spillway?

■ What are the requirements of the filtering system? How many gph does it take to properly operate the filter?

■ Will your feature include fish? If so, how many and what size? A big fish population indicates the need for a biological filter. After deciding on a filter, ask: How many gph are needed to operate the biofilter?

■ If your design includes a fountain, how

Choose from an array of energy-efficient recirculating pumps to power water features and other equipment.

HOW TO INTERPRET PUMP CHARACTERISTICS

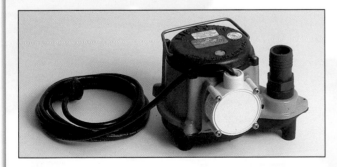

MODEL NUMBER: Identify a pump by the manufacturer's model number. It remains the same from dealer to dealer and helps with comparison shopping.

GPH: Calculate how many gallons per hour (gph) you need, given the horizontal plus vertical distance that recirculating water will flow between the pump and the point where water exits its pipeline.

Purchase a pump with a capacity (gph) that's greater than required.

HEAD (LIFT): The vertical distance that the pump forces water in the line. Horizontal distance is converted to equivalent head at the rate of 10 feet of horizontal distance to 1 foot of vertical lift (head).

MAXIMUM HEAD (LIFT): At the pump's specified maximum head, it no longer recirculates water. Buy a pump with a head height above the total height of the waterfall.

PUMP OUTLET: Where water exits the pump and where the water line is attached to the pump. The pump outlet diameter determines the diameter of the line that carries water from the pump to its discharge point. When the horizontal distance of the line exceeds 15 feet, use a fitting to increase the discharge connection to the next larger pipe size.

AMPS AND WATTS: Calculate the amount of electricity needed and the approximate cost of running a specific pump based on your local utility rates. Generally, higher numbers translate to higher electrical usage and higher operating expense. Here's a formula: watts × 24 hours (in a day) × 30 days (in a month) ÷ 1,000 = number of kilowatts per month × cost per kilowatt hour = total monthly cost of operating a pump.

PUMPS
continued

many gph are required to operate the type and height of fountain you chose?

When buying a pump consider the following:

■ How many gph does it recirculate at the height and horizontal distance required?
■ How much electricity does it use?
■ How long is it guaranteed to last?
■ How much does it cost?

Pumps' power consumption varies so much that an energy-efficient model can save enough electricity to pay for itself in one or two seasons of operation. Compare the amps and wattage of competing pumps to determine relative efficiency of energy consumption. The lower the amps and wattage, the less electricity a pump consumes.

MEASURING GALLONS PER HOUR

As a pump pushes water higher in a vertical pipe, gravity creates increased resistance.

Therefore the gph of a pump decreases as the discharge height (known as head or lift) is increased. The resistance created by forcing water to flow sideways 10 feet is roughly equivalent to the effect of lifting the water 1 foot vertically. If your pump forces water 20 feet horizontally, for example, that translates to 2 feet vertically. Knowing this gph at a designated point tells you if the pump can deliver the quantity of water needed to properly operate a waterfall with the planned spillway's width, depth, and height as well as its distance from the pump.

Manufacturers list how many gph a pump recirculates at 1 foot of lift and at other heights. If the height you need is between two listed heights, estimate what you could reasonably expect. For example, if you need 300 gph released 3 feet above the water's surface, look for a pump rated at least 300 gph at 3 feet of head. That same pump might recirculate only 200 gph at 6 feet of lift. It would not be powerful enough to recirculate 300 gph for a 6-foot-high waterfall.

Measure the water distance vertically from the pump, not from the water's surface, to build in a margin of error. One way or the other, avoid skimping on gph. When determining the proper flow rate for a waterfall or stream, figure 150 gph for each inch of spillway width. This rate provides a ½-inch-thick sheet of water over the falls. You'll also need to know how far the water must travel horizontally in the pipeline. Each 10 feet of horizontal distance creates approximately as much resistance against the pump as 1 foot of head. Consider a pump that must force water 10 feet in a pipe across the pond bottom, then 5 feet up the pipe to the release point in the waterfall. This is equivalent to a 6-foot head.

Although some variation exists from rated gph capacity, pumps do not operate at more than their rated gph capacity for each rated height. To

HOW TO ESTIMATE WATERFALL FLOW

Use a ¾-inch diameter garden hose to test what your new waterfall will look like before investing in a pump for it. This test assumes water pressure at the tap measures 40 to 60 pounds per square inch (normally found in municipal water systems). The hose produces a flow rate of 800 to 900 gph, assuming no nozzle or other restriction. Let the hose discharge at its maximum rate where you plan to have the water line from the pump discharge water. After observing the effect of this rate on your newly constructed waterfall, decide if you want to keep the flow rate at 800 to 900 gph or adjust it higher or lower.

be safe, purchase a pump with greater capacity than estimated need. While a pump's gph cannot be increased, it is easily reduced using a valve on the pipeline or a restrictor clamp on the flexible tubing that limits the flow of water from the pump to the discharge point. Some pumps come with a built-in valve on the discharge. Any restriction you add should be placed on the water line only after the water exits the pump—never before entering the pump. Pumps easily withstand this restriction. It has the same effect as making the pump push the water higher in the line.

THE BEST PUMP FOR YOUR WATER FEATURE

Unless you plan to have an extremely large waterfall or stream, use a submersible pump. Residential water features usually employ submersible pumps of less than 4,000 gph. They provide noiseless operation and ease of setup, giving them a distinct advantage over nonsubmersible pumps. Submersible pumps usually feature a screen intake that protects them from clogging. Some models include a built-in filter and work well for most small fountains, waterfalls, and streams.

Buy the highest-quality pump that you can afford. Bronze, brass, and stainless steel models are top-of-the-line and will withstand heavy use over the years. Cast iron and aluminum pumps offer moderate prices and quality compared to the least-expensive plastic models. Select a pump with a cord that's long enough to reach the nearest ground fault circuit interrupter (GFCI) electrical outlet. If the outlet lacks GFCI protection, use an outdoor extension cord that has a built-in GFCI.

Place a submersible pump on a platform of bricks or flat rocks a few inches above the pond bottom. This keeps the pump above sediment that accumulates on the pond floor and makes it easier to clean the pump.

Choose from oil-filled or magnetically driven submersible pumps. The latter have a longer life than oil-filled pumps and consume substantially less energy per gph than other pumps. Oil-filled pumps are normally required for high head requirements. Beware of the potential of contaminating leaks from oil-filled pumps. Avoid low-priced residential sump pumps, even though they have an attractive gph rating. They typically burn out under continuous operation within a few months.

NONSUBMERSIBLE PUMPS

Use nonsubmersible (external) pumps for large water features using over 12,000 gph

or high-output situations, such as waterfalls, requiring a high lift. Compared to submersible pumps, external models make more noise and cost more to operate, but they're easier to access for maintenance and cost less. A complex plumbing installation may require a professional's assistance. These units must be kept dry and well-ventilated within a protective housing. Be sure to screen the intake to prevent clogging. Other necessities include locating the pump where water flows to it via gravity, or installing a check valve, then priming the pump. Follow the manufacturer's directions for installing and operating your pump.

This nonsubmersible pump is designed to handle the requirements of a system with a biological filter and a waterfall.

TYPICAL FLOW RATES* FOR WATER FEATURES

POND, SMALL: 40 to 400 gph
POND, MEDIUM: 100 to 1,000 gph
POND, LARGE: 400 to 4,000 gph
FOUNTAIN: Varies widely; often 200 to 400 gph. Check the fountain manufacturer's rating.
SPLASHING STATUARY, SMALL: 40 to 150 gph
SPLASHING STATUARY, MEDIUM: 100 to 400 gph
SPLASHING STATUARY, LARGE: 300 to 800 gph
FILTER, BIOLOGICAL: Recirculates 15 to 25 percent of the feature's water volume per hour.
FILTER, MECHANICAL: Recirculates 50 percent of the feature's water volume per hour.
STREAM: Recirculates 50 to 100 percent of the feature's water volume per hour.
WATERFALL: Recirculates 50 to 100 percent of the feature's water volume; 150 gph per inch of spillway width measured at the fall's discharge height.

*Flow rate (gph or gallons per hour) is an essential indicator of which pump to buy. Determine the pump's gph rate in part by taking into account the horizontal and vertical distance from the pump to the point of discharge. Also consider the pond's volume, which includes water in waterfalls and streams. Check the manufacturer's recommendation for any specific feature.

FILTERS

THE NITROGEN CYCLE

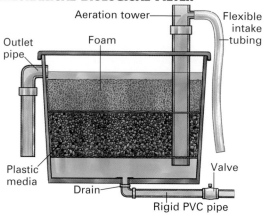

The mechanical part of the filter (foam) strains debris, while the biological part (plastic media) provides a home for beneficial bacteria.

THE NITROGEN CYCLE

The No. 1 question people ask about water gardening is how to keep the pond water from turning green. The short answer is to minimize the number and size of fish in the water feature and to maximize the number of plants. A basic understanding that fish waste stimulates algae growth will help you to better manage your pond water.

The healthy balance of life in your water feature depends on a scientific phenomenon called the nitrogen cycle. This process of nature is as basic to aquatic life as photosynthesis is to plants. Successful pond owners understand how to harness the cycle for their benefit. Ignoring it leads to toxic water with dead fish and scavengers.

Basically here's how the nitrogen cycle works: Fish eat food they find in the water, digest it, and excrete waste. This waste matter contains nitrogen in the form of ammonia. Uneaten fish food and other organic matter (material from plants or animals) likewise contribute nitrogen in the form of ammonia (NH_3). If left unchecked the ammonia becomes deadly to fish and scavengers living in the water.

BENEFICIAL NITRIFYING BACTERIA

As ammonia accumulates in the water, beneficial nitrifying bacteria and enzymes go to work breaking ammonia down into nitrite. These nitrifying critters cling to surface areas all around the pond. They reach significant numbers about the same time the mosslike green algae become noticeable on the sides of the pond. Nitrifying bacteria begin their helpful work in spring as the water temperature rises to 50° F and warmer. They slow down in fall as the water temperature drops below 50° F.

The action of nitrifying bacteria and enzymes that thrive on nitrite oxidizes nitrite to nitrate, a form of nitrogen generally benign to pond creatures and beneficial to plants. Plants take up the nitrate; fish and scavengers nibble on the greenery and return nitrogen to the water, completing the nitrogen cycle.

A COMMON SCENARIO

Released into clear, fresh water, healthy fish sometimes lose their appetite and die for no apparent reason. A water test reveals ammonia in excess of a level safe for fish. That's because during the first four to six weeks of a pond's life, the colony of beneficial bacteria is developing and not yet able to handle the load of fish. Seeding the water with additional beneficial bacteria could have prevented fish kills. So would adding only a few fish at the beginning so that the ammonia level doesn't rise faster than the increasing bacteria population can handle.

Remember that fish food, eaten and uneaten alike, contains nitrogen. The more food you put into the water, the more nitrate results. Algae thrive on nitrate. Unless the water feature grows a sufficient quantity of efficient nitrate users, the algae grow out of control. Limiting the amount of fish food helps reduce the intensity of green water that results from an oversupply of nitrate.

Stop feeding fish when the water temperature drops below 50° F. At this point, the beneficial nitrifying bacteria slack off from their summertime work, and the lower temperatures slow down the decay of organic matter, so the release of toxic ammonia also slows. Overfeeding fish, however, promotes deadly ammonia levels. It's best to allow the pond to reach a natural balance or employ extra help from a biological filter.

People mistakenly believe all green water is bad, but fish thrive in healthy water containing algae. Algae is excessive and needs controlling when you can't see your hand 12 inches beneath the water's surface.

MECHANICAL FILTRATION

When pond water becomes cloudy, filtration offers a solution. Mechanical filtration involves forcing pond water through porous media (usually filter pads) that catches larger particles. Most mechanical filters sit on the bottom of the water feature, but some work outside the pond.

CAPACITY

Do not skimp on the capacity of your mechanical filter. To do so simply wastes money. The pump for a mechanical filter should recirculate the feature's water volume at least once every two hours. A 1,000-gallon water feature needs a pump that can recirculate at least 500 gph through the mechanical filter. Better yet, select a unit designed to function at a slightly higher capacity than you need.

If you choose a mechanical pond filter, make sure it's designed to handle the capacity of your water feature. If you buy a unit with too little capacity or if you fail to clean it regularly, it will be useless. Swimming pool filters become clogged within hours of filtering pond water because they're designed for use with algae-killing chemicals.

The advantages of mechanical filters include their modest cost, ease of setup, and simple maintenance. Disadvantages include frequency of cleaning and lack of ability to eliminate algae.

FILTERS WITH AN ADDED PUMP

Most mechanical filters come without a built-in pump. If the filter doesn't have its own pump, connect one that's appropriate for the size of the water feature.

Use a pump (with a minimum gph of half the feature's water volume) that can be connected to the filter using flexible vinyl tubing. Attach the filter to the pump's intake

A mechanical filter with a built-in pump strains particles of dirt and other matter that pass through it and adds oxygen to the water for healthier fish.

(where water is drawn into the pump). Before you attach the tubing to the pump's intake or discharge, remove the pump's screen or prefilter unit, which covers the intake and is designed to prevent clogging of the pump by keeping out leaves, twigs, and such. Do not attempt to take the pump apart—that would void the warranty.

FILTERS WITH A BUILT-IN PUMP

Some mechanical filters include a recirculating pump. One type of mechanical filtration unit features a pump built into the bottom half of the filter box. The top half consists of two foam filters, one on top of the other. The bottom filter pad rests on a perforated shelf that allows filtered water into the lower chamber. The pump then discharges the filtered water either directly into the pond or into flexible tubing to power a waterfall or decorative fountain.

Some mechanical filters operate outside the pond, making cleaning easier. In this case, the water goes first to the pump, which forces the water through tubing to the exterior mechanical filter. The newly filtered water then flows under pressure to a waterfall or stream, or directly into the pond. Before starting this type of filtration system, attach tubing to the pump's discharge and run it to the intake of the filter unit. Then run tubing from the filter outlet to flow into the pond, stream, or waterfall.

Freshly filtered water splashes over a waterfall and returns to the pond. Including plants around the edges of a waterfall helps prevent erosion.

FILTERS
continued

The resistance of the filter reduces the volume of water that the pump recirculates. If for any reason the gph drops too low, the filter's effectiveness is reduced. By the same token, if a filter becomes clogged and a pump's intake is restricted, the pump could be damaged.

Aim to recirculate half the water in the pond once per hour or all the water once every two hours. If the pump powers a waterfall 3 feet above the water surface directly above it, the pump should be rated to recirculate at least half the pond water once per hour at the 3-foot head.

FILTER MAINTENANCE

Mechanical filters usually work out of sight, on the pond bottom. But placing the filter in an easy-to-reach location saves time and effort for the busy owner. If the pond is so deep its bottom cannot easily be reached, consider making a platform for the filter using clean bricks or flat rocks.

You will soon learn to recognize when the filter needs cleaning. Reduced water flow indicates that the filter is clogged with debris. Clean the filter daily during warm summer periods. Be sure that clamps hold the tubing tightly to the filter unit and the pump. Efficiency is lost when water leaks at these points, whether the pump is located inside or outside the pond.

BIOLOGICAL FILTRATION

Biological filtration occurs naturally in water features where plants and naturally occurring bacteria maintain water quality without

Biofilters enable extra fish to live in a pond. The filters house additional beneficial bacteria that neutralize toxic fish waste.

supplemental filtration. Biofilters work to make water clear and healthy for fish. They work partly as mechanical filters, trapping suspended debris from pond water. In addition, nitrifying bacteria and enzymes inside the biofilter remove ammonia and nitrites from the water.

Various biofilters are popular among koi hobbyists and ornamental fish dealers. Generally, biofilters are efficient and easy to clean. Every month or two, you'll need to rinse off one-fourth to one-third of the elements (more than that interferes with the effectiveness of the nitrifying bacteria). The disadvantages of biofilters include their initial cost, complicated installation, and bulk (which makes them difficult to conceal).

HOW BIOFILTERS WORK

Filter manufacturers search for ways to maximize the number of nitrifying bacteria and enzymes in a filter unit. These beneficial microscopic creatures spend their lives clinging to any stationary aquatic surface, so filter designers employ elements with as much surface area as possible, such as gravel, volcanic rock, and many imaginative configurations of plastic.

Although the bacteria require oxygen to function, water typically comes into the biofilter from near the bottom of the pond where oxygen levels are low. To remedy this deficiency, better-quality biofilters aerate the water before it reaches the nitrifying bacteria. Aeration yields a denser population of bacteria, which in turn allows a more compact housing for the filter.

Beneficial bacteria in a biological filter cling to surface areas of media in the unit's chamber and consume suspended matter and nutrients that pass through the filter.

Some biofilters include a space for aquatic plants that absorb nitrogen from nitrates and nitrites as well as ammonia. When planted, the filter robs algae of the nutrients they need to thrive, thus enhancing water quality.

Use a water test kit to measure the ammonia or nitrate levels. A biological filter is needed if they test too high. Too high a reading results from having a greater fish population than can be handled by the nitrifying bacteria and enzymes naturally found in the pond.

ABOVEGROUND BIOLOGICAL FILTERS

Most biofilters are designed to operate above the ground outside the pond. The pump sends pond water up to the aboveground filter unit. First it is aerated before flowing through the mechanical, debris-removal section. Then it flows through the high-surface section housing the concentrated nitrifying bacteria and enzyme colonies, and they detoxify the water. With some units, the water passes a final sector of aquatic plants where nutrient removal reduces algae growth. The purified water then flows out of the unit.

IN-GROUND BIOLOGICAL FILTERS

Larger ponds, especially koi ponds, frequently utilize in-ground biofilters. Often made of high-density polyethylene, they typically feature round chambers and conical bottoms. A typical unit sits in the ground with its top slightly above water level. A nonsubmersible pump draws water through piping from the pond's bottom drain. At the same time, the pump pulls filtered water from the chambers of the biofilter.

Easy-to-clean, pressurized biofilters are available for small ponds. As small, in-ground units, they're accessible and easy to hide with imitation (fiberglass) rocks.

PRESSURIZED BIOLOGICAL FILTERS

Also known as bead filters, these units operate within a pressurized housing. A high-pressure, nonsubmersible pump draws water from the pond, usually through bottom drains. A pressurized vortex at the pump's intake removes heavy suspended matter from the water. The pump forces the pond water into the filter, where nitrifying bacteria and enzymes flourish on beads designed to have high surface area. The filtration media collect suspended matter in the spaces between the beads. The slow water flow over the huge surface area provided by the beads allow

BUBBLE-WASHED BEAD FILTER

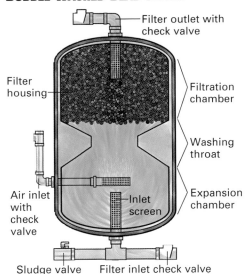

Filter outlet with check valve / Filter housing / Filtration chamber / Washing throat / Air inlet with check valve / Inlet screen / Expansion chamber / Sludge valve / Filter inlet check valve

A bead filter clarifies water by trapping debris. It also works as a biofilter: The beads provide a place for beneficial bacteria to flourish.

excellent colonization of the bacteria and enzymes. Purified water forced out of the pressurized filter housing then goes to a waterfall or into the pond.

A pressure gauge on the intake valve indicates that the filter needs cleaning by showing pressure increases. A decrease in the volume of water coming out of the filter also indicates that the unit needs cleaning. Back flushing for a few minutes does the job. Top-of-the-line units include a propeller to loosen the beads, which sometimes become impacted.

PLANT FILTERS

Plant filters make the nitrogen cycle work to your advantage through a simple concept: Pond water filters through an aquatic plant bed, allowing plants to do the work. If you want to make a plant filter, such as a bog, include it as part of the pond construction. By integrating a plant filter into your water feature, you'll enjoy the plants' ornamental qualities as well as their filtering abilities.

HOW PLANT FILTERS WORK

Nitrifying bacteria and enzymes colonize the gravel bed of the plant filter. Gravel serves as a mechanical filter that removes debris from the pond water. Bacteria and enzymes reduce ammonia in the water to nitrite and then to nitrate. Water-loving marginal or bog plants flourish in the shallow, nitrate-rich water. Most of the suspended matter carried in by the water disintegrates. The gravel filter bed is big enough to function for years without becoming clogged.

FILTERS
continued

A bog garden, created at one end of a pond, functions as a plant filter, improving the water quality in the pond. It also accommodates water-loving plants that might not grow elsewhere.

DESIGNING A PLANT FILTER

Whatever surface area you plan for a new pond, make the plant filter area about 25 percent of that figure. For example, when designing a pond with 120 square feet of surface area, figure an additional surface area of 30 square feet for the plant filter.

Although a dam-type barrier or wall will separate the pond and the plant filter, figure that your pond's flexible liner will cover both areas (see page 11). First, figure the dimensions of pond liner required for the pond. Then figure the dimensions needed for the adjacent plant filter using the same method of calculating as for the pond. When the two imaginary rectangles are placed side by side, calculate the combined dimensions to determine the liner dimensions.

SAMPLE CALCULATIONS

For example, consider the calculations for the 120-square-foot pond with a plant filter. A 10 × 12-foot pond would use a 10 × 3-foot plant filter. The pond, if 2 feet deep, needs a 16 × 18-foot liner. The 1-foot-deep plant filter needs a 14 × 7-foot portion of liner. One liner covering both parts measures 16 × 25 feet. Because many suppliers offer 15 × 25-foot liners, the budget-oriented pond design might shrink to 10 × 11 feet (the plant filter surface remains 10 × 3 feet).

The pond contains approximately 1,500 gallons of water. Recirculating the volume of water approximately every five hours through the plant filter to achieve clear water calls for a submersible pump capable of producing 300 gph at the discharge point.

PLANT FILTER INSTALLATION

Excavate your pond in the usual manner, except that along one side dig a plant filter 12 inches deep and 3 feet wide (as in the example below left), or as wide as desired. With treated lumber or concrete blocks, build a 6- to 12-inch-thick dam between the pond and the plant filter. Water from the plant filter will spill over the wall into the pond. (A 2½-inch-wide spillway would result in a ¼-inch flow of water returning to the pond; water would only trickle over a 5-inch-wide spillway.) Drape the liner over the spillway and top it with flat rocks. Secure the rocks with mortar to make a walkway.

Next, attach tubing to the pump at the far side and run it to the plant filter, where it will attach to 1½-inch-wide PVC pipe with ⅜-inch holes drilled 12 inches apart. Use one length of the pipe for each 3 feet of filter width. Use a PVC T-piece or elbow fittings when a manifold is needed to distribute the water into more than one pipe under the plant filter.

Cover the PVC pipe with landscape fabric, which allows water to pass out of the pipe but prevents particles less than ⅜ inch from entering the pipe. Cover the fabric with rinsed ⅜- to 1½-inch gravel to within 2 inches of the spillway. Rinsing gravel before you fill the pond prevents dust from forming an unwanted film on the water surface. Now you're ready to plant.

Push aside the gravel to make planting holes for the root balls of bog plants. If you purchase bare-root plants, pot them in perforated containers before setting the plants in the bog. Space marginal plants, such as cattails and iris, 18 inches apart.

PLANT FILTER

Water filtered by plants in the bog area flows through a pipe laid under the capstone and into the pond.

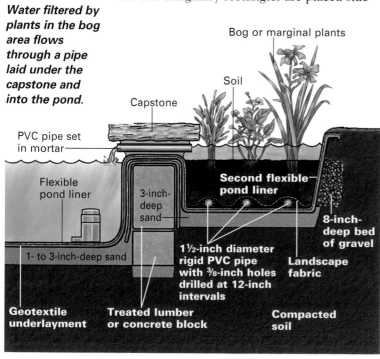

BOTTOM DRAINS AND BULKHEAD CONNECTIONS

Bottom drains and bulkhead connectors are specialized pipe fittings that allow a watertight passageway for water or power lines to go through a pond liner below the water surface.

A bottom drain allows you to let the water flow out the bottom of your water feature by disconnecting the pump and turning a valve. A bulkhead connection is a specialized fitting on the side of a water feature into which you screw a pipe or pipe fitting. Guard against leaks by following manufacturer's directions carefully when installing a bottom drain or a bulkhead connection.

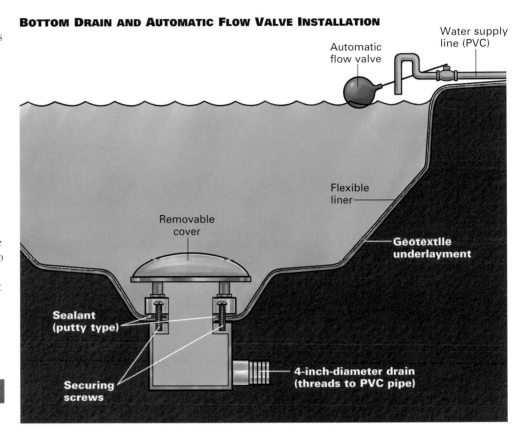

BOTTOM DRAIN AND AUTOMATIC FLOW VALVE INSTALLATION

Automatic flow valve

Water supply line (PVC)

Removable cover

Flexible liner

Geotextile underlayment

Sealant (putty type)

Securing screws

4-inch-diameter drain (threads to PVC pipe)

BOTTOM DRAINS

Ponds stocked heavily with fish, especially koi, often include one or more bottom drains. A bottom drain made for koi ponds works just as successfully in water gardens, particularly if stocked heavily with fish. Koi keepers regularly replace 10 percent or more of their pond water. Drains make this easier to do. Installing a 4-inch-diameter drainpipe greatly reduces the likelihood of clogging.

Bottom drains include a removable cover that minimizes suction created as the water drains. This helps to prevent small fish and large debris from passing through and clogging the bottom drain. The drains also include watertight fittings that clamp against a flexible liner or a rigid shell liner. Bottom drains work well in concrete ponds too.

Swimming pool drains are too fine and quickly become clogged in a fishpond or water-garden environment. Some filter systems are designed to receive water from the pool bottom, thus making a bottom drain necessary for them.

BULKHEAD CONNECTIONS

The bulkhead connector is a short length of flanged, externally threaded pipe equipped

with a locknut and rubber washer for making a watertight seal. The inside of the pipe is either threaded to accept a variety of pipe fittings or smooth for solvent welding of PVC pipe. The diameter of the pipe that runs through the wall determines what diameter bulkhead connector you need. The uses of a bulkhead connector include passage for electrical power, overflow water, intake water, or recirculated water for a filter, waterfall, stream, UV clarifier, statuary, or fountainhead.

Most water features don't include either a bottom drain or a bulkhead connector. The submersible pump that regularly recirculates the water works well to drain the pond for maintenance. Typically, the water and power lines of a water feature (including many koi ponds) run into the pond between the edging material and the top of the liner, whether the liner is flexible, rigid, or concrete. Cutting a flexible liner or a preformed shell may void the manufacturer's guarantee. What's more, cutting a hole in your liner, even for a bottom drain or bulkhead, increases the chance of a leak.

PIPES AND FITTINGS

Today's professionals and amateurs prefer plastic pipe, tubing, fittings, and valves. Their ease of installation, longevity, noncorrosiveness, and nontoxic properties make plastic piping and other supplies ideal for water features.

Flexible vinyl tubing is the least expensive and quickest to install for a water line. If the size of the line you need exceeds a 1-inch inside dimension (ID), use flexible PVC tubing, which is more expensive but easy to install. For 2-inch lines or larger, use rigid PVC pipe. It costs less than flexible PVC. Rigid PVC resists being squeezed by traffic or the weight of the material that is placed over it.

Use galvanized or bronze supplies if you can't find plastic. Avoid copper. It's expensive, it deteriorates in acidic soil or water, and it requires a plumber to install.

FLEXIBLE TUBING AND PIPING

Flexible vinyl tubing has various uses for plumbing water features. Attach one end of the tubing to a pump and attach its other end to the equipment that the pump operates, such as a fountain, waterfall, filter, UV clarifier, or statuary. Or carefully let the line discharge into a waterway basin—the pool of water that overflows at the top of a waterfall. The job might also be more complex. For example, you may attach the line to a UV clarifier and continue with another section of tubing to a filter that empties into a waterfall basin.

Secure a hose clamp around tubing wherever it connects with any equipment to keep it in place and ensure a watertight connection. Match the clamp size to the tubing; use a ½-inch clamp for a ½-inch OD pipe, for example.

When connected to a submersible pump, flexible tubing makes it easier to lift the pump for inspection or service. Given a choice, thicker tubing resists kinking and squeezing better than thinner-walled tubing. Avoid bending flexible tubing around a corner, burying it underground, or using it in other ways that would restrict the water flowing through it.

Avoid clear tubing. Wherever sunlight reaches the plastic, it encourages the growth of algae inside it, which eventually clogs the tubing. Choose black tubing instead; it blocks light and prevents algae accumulation.

Flexible, schedule-40 PVC tubing works well for water features. Its flexibility allows the line to run without flow-restricting

elbows, yet it's strong enough to resist buckling when covered with soil. Use flexible PVC pipe glue to secure connections.

Nonkinking corrugated vinyl tubing bends around corners without crimping. Like standard corrugated tubing, it has a wavy exterior, but the smooth interior won't slow water flow. Use clamps with foam strips on the inside that correspond to the ridges and valleys of the corrugated material to create a watertight connection to a pump, filter, clarifier, fountain, or other equipment. This tubing functions well when buried up to 6 inches deep. Use barbed (also called push-in or compression) fittings, which simply push together to link flexible piping; use plastic or stainless steel clamps to secure the connections.

RIGID PIPING

Rigid PVC pipe is corrosion-resistant, lightweight, and inexpensive. Use schedule-40 PVC pipe to avoid the drawbacks of flexible tubing. Rigid PVC resists compression under the weight of soil, rocks, or foot traffic. In addition, algae doesn't grow inside the opaque white pipe. Choose rigid pipe for runs of 15 to 20 feet or longer, for a water volume of 3,000 gph or more, and for situations where the pipe must be buried underground. Elbows, available in 45- and 90-degree turns, allow a change in the direction of PVC pipe and water flow without significantly reducing the flow.

Make a rigid water line by cutting lengths of pipe to match the layout you design. Lengths of PVC pipe cut easily with a hacksaw. Then glue the pieces together. Use PVC pipe glue to make a watertight connection. Other connection options include threaded fittings (screw) and compression fittings (push). Use Teflon tape on threaded pipe connections to make them watertight. Carefully inspect and flow-test all connections to make certain they don't leak.

TUBING AND PIPING SIZE

Pipe diameter is determined by the flow (gph) necessary to operate the filter, waterfall, or other features. When buying piping or tubing, increase the diameter to the next larger size when the needed length exceeds 15 feet. A larger diameter reduces friction of water against the piping, reduces pressure against the pump, and helps to maintain the desired gph. The size of the piping or tubing you use must match the connection piece (either the discharge or intake) on the pump. For example, buy 1-inch ID tubing if the pump volute (outlet) measures 1-inch OD. If you

Flexible tubing

Lay-flat discharge hose

Schedule 40, rigid PVC pipe

Clear, flexible tubing

Kink-free corrugated vinyl piping and fittings

have 1-inch OD tubing for the pump, use a reducer-type fitting to connect the pump and tubing. In the case of a pump that takes a 1-inch PVC pipe that would be more than 15 feet long, use 1¼-inch-diameter piping. Use a reducer connection to make the larger pipe compatible with the pump volute.

ASSORTED FITTINGS

Fittings allow you to regulate, direct, and secure the flow of water through the piping or tubing. Flexible tubing or a hand-tight PVC union makes pump removal quick and easy. If the pump has a threaded female socket and you want to connect it to vinyl tubing, use a polyethylene barb fitting and clamp to do the job. Use standard-socket PVC fittings for PVC pipe and tubing.

BALL VALVE: A fast on-off valve, this water flow regulator operates with a one-quarter turn of the handle to stop or start the water stream. Inside is a ball with a hole in it. When the hole is aligned with the pipe, water flows through it; when rotated away from the the water flow, the ball blocks the water.

GATE VALVE: Where you'll need to make minor flow adjustments, use a gate valve. Turning the handle raises or lowers a barrier (the gate). When raised, water flows freely; when lowered completely, it stops the water flow. You can open or close the gate to any size opening to adjust water flow.

KNIFE VALVE: Knife valves, also called slide valves, are often used to control water flow to drain lines, filters, and skimmers. Pulling up or pushing down on the handle, rapidly shuts off the water for servicing this equipment.

THREE-WAY OR DIVERTER VALVE: This water flow regulator has one inlet and two outlets. Changes in the valve handle position alter the balance of flow between the two outlets. Use it when one pump is operating two features, such as a filter and a fountain.

GLOBE VALVE: The globe valve is too restrictive because it requires a pressure far higher (40 to 60 pounds per square inch) than is generated by water-feature pumps.

CHECK VALVE: Permits water to pass in one direction, but stops it if it starts to move back in the opposite direction. Install a check valve on the line between the water and a nonsubmersible pump not fed by gravity. Otherwise when the pump stops, air gets into the line, and the pump loses its prime.

HOSE CLAMP: Holds flexible tubing or piping securely to a pump or to statuary.

HOSE RESTRICTOR CLAMP: Tightens on flexible tubing to reduce excessive water flow and secure a connection.

FLANGED TANK ADAPTER (BULKHEAD CONNECTOR): A fitting that enables a water line to pass out of the water feature below the water's surface while preventing the feature from leaking where the lines penetrate the wall.

T-FITTINGS AND Y-FITTINGS: These direct a stream of water to divide into two lines.

ELBOWS: Make 45- and 90-degree turns in rigid or flexible pipelines.

ADAPTERS: Various kinds make it possible to join rigid pipe to flexible tubing. Socket weld PVC fittings to male/female threaded connections.

REDUCER: Features a different diameter at each end to connect piping of differing diameters.

AUTOMATIC FLOW VALVE: Ensures that, despite evaporation, the water in a pond, stream, or other feature remains at the desired level. It works like the float valve in a toilet. When working properly, the automatic flow valve masks a leak that might develop in the pond. If the flow valve malfunctions, the feature may overflow with chlorinated tap water, killing the aquatic life in the pond. If it fails to add water while you're away, the water depth could become dangerously low, adversely affecting plants, fish, scavengers, and equipment. (See the illustration on page 29 for an example of how these valves work.)

1. ball valve;
2. 1-inch-diameter gate valve;
3. check valve;
4. 1-inch-diameter gate valve;
5. diverter valve;
6. T-fitting;
7. reducer;
8. Y-fitting;
9. hose clamps;
10. restrictor clamp; and
11. adapter.

SKIMMERS

A skimmer removes fallen leaves and other floating debris from the water. Include a skimmer in your plans when using the clear-water approach to pond construction.

A skimmer prevents problems associated with leaves and other debris that fall into your water feature and present a hazard to your fish. As leaves decay and sink, they consume oxygen and produce toxic gases that escape harmlessly into the atmosphere. This isn't a problem until winter, when ice forms on the pond, trapping the gases and killing the fish.

A skimmer removes floating matter before it decays and sinks. It helps the water quality by increasing the oxygen level as the skimmed water splashes back into the pond.

HOW A SKIMMER WORKS

The skimmer functions as a mechanical filter that sits at the edge of a water feature. A lid on the skimmer top allows access for weekly cleaning. The top of the skimmer typically sits about 1½ inches above the surface of the water; if the water level in your feature drops too low, the skimmer sucks air instead of water. Netting within the skimmer traps debris. A pump inside the device works constantly to draw the water into it. Water from the skimmer is then pumped to a filter, waterfall, or other location and recirculates back into the pond.

PLAN AHEAD

A skimmer works best when installed downwind, allowing prevailing winds to direct leaves and other material toward the skimmer. Recirculated water should re-enter the pond at the opposite side from the skimmer. You increase the skimmer's efficiency by locating it opposite the waterfall or stream, as the steady current of water entering the pond also propels floating debris toward the skimmer.

There are some negatives to using a skimmer. While collecting unwanted floating debris, the skimmer may also draw in floating plants. In addition, it sucks in fish, especially little ones, and traps frogs and tadpoles. Check it daily and rescue any trapped pond denizens.

A skimmer requires extra planning to conceal it, and extra plumbing is required to move water from the skimmer to the far side of the feature, so you'll have to incorporate other equipment, such as a filter or fountain, along the same plumbing path to increase efficiency. A skimmer also increases installation investment and adds to operating expense.

If desired, include an automatic flow valve with a pond skimmer to help maintain the appropriate water level.

SKIMMER AND PLANT FILTER INSTALLATION

The skimmer's overflow pipe should slope away from the unit to prevent water from entering the skimmer during heavy rains.

Bog or marginal plants

Overflow pipe

Removable lid

Skimmer

Grate

Submersible pump

Flexible liner

Geotextile underlayment　Sand

Rigid PVC pipe

Sand

Perforated PVC pipe

UV clarifier (optional)

ULTRAVIOLET CLARIFIERS AND MAGNETIC ALGAE CONTROLLERS

If you are looking for a surefire way to avoid green water due to algae, you'll find it with an ultraviolet (UV) clarifier. Also known as an ultraviolet sterilizer, this device kills suspended algae (planktonic algae), bacteria, and other microorganisms as they flow through the clarifier. A UV clarifier also kills fungi and some parasites that attack fish.

A clarifier kills beneficial organisms only if they get into the UV chamber, but it won't affect the beneficial bacteria that colonize inside the biofilter and on the sides and bottom of the pond. Aquatic plants should be included in a plan that uses a UV clarifier. Otherwise you'll end up with clear water that's full of nitrites, which can be detrimental to fish.

HOW A UV CLARIFIER WORKS

A UV clarifier consists of an ultraviolet bulb inside a quartz-glass tube and a PVC housing. A pump forces water through a pipe to the UV unit which sits outside of the pond. The water is irradiated as it passes between the inside of the housing and the outside of the glass tube. (The light breaks down algae.) The water is then returned directly to the pond, or it returns there via a biofilter or a waterfall, stream, fountain, piped statuary, or bog.

UV clarifiers are labeled according to their wattage, maximum gph, and recommended pond size range. Their strength varies. If the maximum flow rate for the UV clarifier is exceeded, algae will move past the UV light too quickly to be killed. Buy a clarifier with a maximum gph capacity that exceeds the gph of the pump that powers water to it. A higher wattage means that the unit can successfully handle a greater gph. Plug the unit into a 120-volt outdoor outlet with a GFCI.

Because clarifiers kill bacteria, remember to unplug the UV unit when adding beneficial bacteria to a biofilter or directly into the pond. Resume operating it when you want to rid the water of suspended algae. A UV lightbulb is good for a single season, so replace it each spring. Even if the light continues to burn for a new season, its spectrum will have changed and will no longer be effective.

MAGNETIC ALGAE CONTROLLER

This device works to rid the pond of filamentous algae, the kind that adheres to the walls and bottom of the pond, as well as to objects within the pond. A magnetic algae controller also reduces the lime buildup on the quartz tube of a UV clarifier, which improves its effectiveness. The device works only in ponds when the pH is 7.5 or lower. Filamentous algae require the presence of carbon ions to adhere to pond surfaces. Magnets in the unit alter the nature of the ions so that the algae cannot adhere to pond surfaces. Water passes through the unit with no external power required.

An alternate type requires 120-volt standard household power that is reduced to 12 volts by a step-down transformer. Circulated water passes through piping outside the water feature. Electromagnetic units clamped onto the piping modify the carbon ions.

A properly sized UV clarifier (sterilizer) ensures no green water in your feature.

Magnetic algae controllers can prevent the buildup of surface-clinging algae when the pH is under 7.5.

UV CLARIFIER

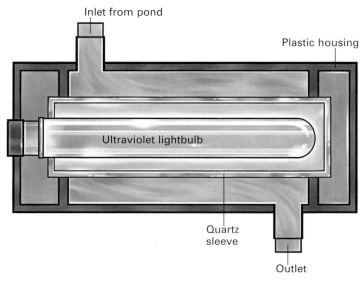

Inlet from pond

Plastic housing

Ultraviolet lightbulb

Quartz sleeve

Outlet

ELECTRICAL POWER

You can successfully operate an ecologically balanced water feature without using electrical power. But most water feature owners prefer to add the visual, aural, and biological benefits that moving, splashing, pump-powered water provides. Other pond accessories require electricity as well. Outdoor lighting enables homeowners to view their gardens in the evening and at night. Fishkeepers in cold regions rely on deicers to safeguard their prized fish during winter.

Solar energy or batteries can power pumps and lights. But solar-powered pumps don't work on cloudy days and at night. A submersible pump quickly consumes the energy stored in a battery. Standard household 120-volt alternating current supplies most of the power for today's water features and their accessories; 120-volt or 12-volt power runs most outdoor lighting systems.

Before starting any electrical installation, learn about your local electrical code from your city or county inspector (department of building inspection). Also check the National Electric Code (NEC), which gives minimum standards for outdoor wiring. Local building codes may have particular requirements, depending on climate and soil conditions. For example, your local code may require underground power lines to be encased in conduit buried at a certain depth.

SAFETY FIRST

Low-voltage systems are easy and safe to install. The potential danger of 120-volt power, however, requires strict attention to safety. Working on electrical lines can be life-threatening if you're not extremely careful, especially around water or moisture. Be certain power is turned off, and double-check it with a voltage meter. If you're not completely comfortable about doing electrical work, hire an electrician.

For safety's sake, install a ground fault circuit interrupter (GFCI, also called a GFI) in each electrical outlet when you plan to use electricity in or near water. In homes with modern wiring, you'll commonly find GFCI electrical outlets in kitchens and bathrooms. The GFCI senses any electrical contact with water. If contact occurs, the GFCI stops the flow of electricity. If pump wiring, even above-ground, becomes frayed and water

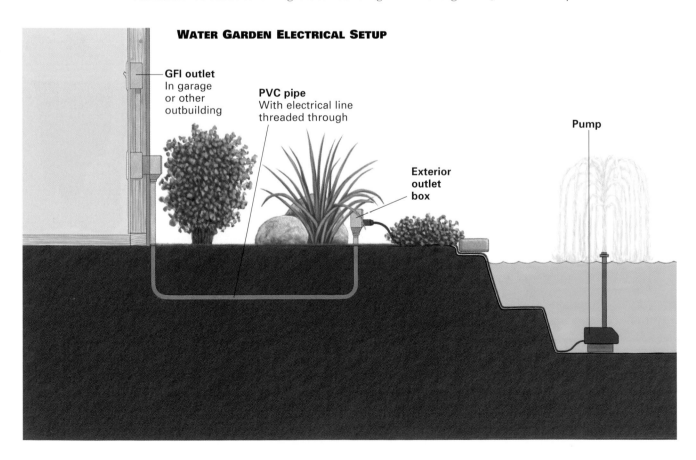

WATER GARDEN ELECTRICAL SETUP

GFI outlet
In garage
or other
outbuilding

PVC pipe
With electrical line
threaded through

**Exterior
outlet
box**

Pump

touches the power wire, the electricity is cut off. Installing a GFCI circuit requires professional-level skills. A less-expensive alternative would be to install a GFCI outlet near the water feature.

Determine the electrical load needed to operate your planned water feature and all of its components. Pumps and other devices are labeled by the manufacturer as having a certain number of watts or amps. Compare the needed power requirements with the number of amps or watts a circuit can handle. Residential circuit breakers handle 15 or 20 amps per circuit for 1,800 watts to 2,400 watts. Figure amps (current) × volts (potential) = watts (power). For the vast majority of residential water features, a single 20-amp circuit suffices. If your watts are expected to exceed 2,400, and you need 20 amps or more, install a second circuit to your breaker box. A large nonsubmersible pump might require a 220-volt circuit, which calls for its own dedicated power line from the circuit breaker. Leave such an installation to an electrician.

ELECTRICAL LINE INSTALLATION

Remember to call your local phone, gas, cable, and electricity providers and ask them to locate and mark all underground utility lines on your property before digging. If possible, when laying new electrical lines underground, avoid traversing any area with a septic system, paving, a deck, a patio, or an outbuilding.

Run the power line through a PVC schedule-40 pipe buried at least 18 inches deep. At this depth, the line is less likely to be damaged by digging near it. Consider installing an electrical switch in the house or on a porch with a waterproof outdoor switch to control the lights or other equipment for your water feature.

INSTALLING A POWER BOX OR OUTLET

Ensure the safe and proper installation of a weatherproof GFCI-protected power outlet or a separate box (metal or plastic) by following local building codes. These may specify its location in relation to the water feature as well as the appropriate choice of materials. In addition, determine where the pump and other electrical equipment will be located,

because their power cords should reach the outlet without the use of extension cords.

Set the power box or outlet on short lengths of galvanized pipe by screwing the pipes into openings at the bottom of the box or outlet and securing each with a bushing. Dig a trench as deep as code requires from your home's nearest power box to the location of the new outdoor box or outlet. Run the power line from the breaker panel of your home through rigid metal or schedule-40 PVC pipe and into the outlet or box. For long-term support and stability, attach the pipes to a 2×6 pressure-treated post with metal brackets. Prepare an 18-inch-deep hole for the support post; then pour concrete into the hole around the post. To avoid inadvertent tripping of the circuit by rain, dew, or sprinklers, install a deep box-type outlet cover to shelter the power cords when they're plugged in.

Where power and fixture wires join, a cover allows access while enclosing the junction, keeping it water tight.

LIGHTING

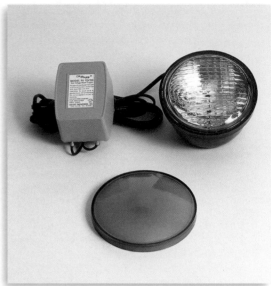

Tuck economical, easy-to-install 12-volt landscape lights in strategic places to illuminate plants or the edge of a water feature.

Low-voltage submersible lights provide safe and attractive options for creating dramatic effects, and they are practical in or out of the water.

Lighting extends your enjoyment of a water feature. You might choose bright, high-intensity halogen lights that virtually turn night into day, or you may prefer subtle, low-voltage lighting that adds mystery and romance to the evening garden. A hanging light or a wall light draws attention to an otherwise unseen container water garden. Strategically placed spotlights, angled to shine high or low, highlight special features. Soft pathway lights help guide visitors around an area. Edge the perimeter of a water feature with gentle highlights that reflect off the water's surface and dance on the ripples of a waterfall. Create a lively, carnival-like atmosphere by installing brightly colored lenses over the lights—but use color sparingly to avoid garishness.

Illuminate a waterfall with an inner glow or add drama to a fountain using submersible lighting. Submersible lights come with their own platform so that they can be moved about the pond floor to satisfy changing requirements. They function best when the water is clear; light dissipates in murky water, accentuating the fact that it's not clear.

After measuring and carefully planning what you want to accomplish with lighting, you have two choices for powering it: low-voltage or line-voltage (120-volt) outdoor lighting. Any lighting placed in or near the water feature should be connected to a GFCI outlet for safety (see page 34).

LOW-VOLTAGE OUTDOOR LIGHTING

Low-voltage lights offer many advantages. They're easy to install and change, use less energy than 120-volt lighting, don't require complicated precautions or configurations, give you more flexibility in your lighting options, and are intrinsically safe. Their initial cost is modest compared to alternatives. Installation of a low-voltage lighting system does not require the services of a licensed electrician; it's a simple do-it-yourself project. Often used with residential water features, low-voltage lights require an electrical transformer that converts regular household 120-volt current into safer 12-volt power. The lights and transformer are sold in handy kits as well as by additional modular pieces. Here's what you'll need: a transformer, a power cable, stakes for in-ground placement, holders for in-water placement, a set of lights, a set of 12-volt bulbs, and optional colored lenses. Some kits include a timer that turns the lights on and off daily. Check the wattage of the transformer to determine the maximum number of lights it can support. You may want to add more lights later without having to buy another transformer.

Consider your options, then decide the location of each light. Take careful measurements so that you can determine which components or kit you need. Follow the instructions that come with the kit or

Well-positioned submersible lights offer an extra dimension for nighttime enjoyment of your water feature, especially when you maintain water clarity.

lighting pieces. Setup usually involves attaching a low-voltage cable to the transformer, laying the cable, and attaching a light at each point along the cable where desired. Plug the transformer into a GFCI outlet when you want to turn on the lights. For wiring simplicity, install a transformer with a built-in timer.

LINE-VOLTAGE LIGHTING

Large, deep pools generally require the more intense light that comes from line-voltage (120-volt) lighting. Although it has the power to provide brilliant lighting, line-voltage lighting can be used for the same purposes as low-voltage lighting. Enlist an electrical contractor or swimming pool contractor to install submersible lights into the walls of a concrete pool.

Remember to include lighting needs when planning power requirements for your water feature. Local regulations often require the services of a licensed electrician to install any 120-volt power line and fixtures connected directly into it. Use only equipment designed for outdoor or underwater use. Fixtures, wire, and other components approved by the Underwriters Laboratories are labeled with a UL seal, indicating that they meet standards and can be used in or near a water feature.

TIPS FOR SUCCESSFUL LIGHTING

1. Install underwater lights directly below a waterfall or fountain. Aim light in the same direction as the water's motion to highlight it.
2. Install ground lighting so that it shines away from the observer. Pathway lights should focus on the ground or nearby plants or ornaments and present no visual glare.
3. Low-voltage underwater bulbs are typically 20 watts; low-voltage garden lightbulbs are usually 10 or 12 watts, and the underwater and garden bulbs may be used interchangeably. However, if you were using a low-voltage garden light set that powered six ground lights

and decided to add one underwater light, you would have to cut back to only four of the ground lights to avoid overloading the circuit.
4. Avoid directing lights to shine on the water's surface—this creates glare. Use the water as a reflecting pool by leaving the surface dark and lighting the surrounding landscaping instead.
5. Periodic cleaning of submersible light lenses keeps them performing at their best.
6. Install lighting around your water feature before you do final landscaping, such as laying sod or adding mulch or gravel.
7. Spotlighting an unusual specimen

such as a night-blooming tropical water lily shows off its special attraction. Avoid spotlighting a night bloomer from below; more subtle side lighting works better.
8. If a low-voltage light fails to work when you test the set, make certain that there is contact with the power cable.
9. Mount the transformer to a vertical stake that is set in concrete for stability.
10. Low-voltage lighting works best in small gardens because each lamp lights a small area. Standard-voltage systems prove more valuable in areas where brilliant illumination is required for safety or security.

DECORATIVE FEATURES

A thin stream of water arching across the pond creates a striking effect while providing fish with extra oxygen. The fountain requires a small submersible pump.

FOUNTAINS AND STATUARY

Thrusting, falling, and splashing water inevitably attracts any viewer's attention. Besides being visually appealing, fountains and piped statuary entrance the ears with music that water makes. Fountainhead designers use their creative skills to provide pond owners with a wide variety of spray patterns, from gentle bubblers and thin columns to spinners and geysers. Statuary choices range from imitations of classical subjects to abstract modern forms. The sight and sound of these water movers greatly enhance the already compelling nature of any water feature. Whatever the landscape style, formal or informal, you can install a fountain or statuary that blends pleasingly with it.

A fountain works as water is forced through the air and falls into a pool or other basin. A fountainhead, situated on the end of a pipe, creates a spray pattern. Fountainhead kits are available in packages that include a pump, connecting piping, and various fountainheads.

Follow the manufacturer's recommendation when choosing an appropriate pump for your fountain. Match the gph range of the pump with the requirement of the fountainhead; also determine the fountainhead's spray height. Take into account that the gph of a pump diminishes if it is located at a distance away from the fountainhead. The distance between the fountainhead and the nearest edge of the water feature represents the maximum desired height of the spray. Beyond being an issue of proportion, this rule has the practical effect of reducing the spray splashing out of the pond onto nearby areas, especially on windy days. The higher the spray, the greater likelihood of making adjacent walkways dangerously slippery, or accidentally draining the pool.

Fountainheads usually connect to a submersible pump, a diverter valve, or a pipe that connects to the pump. If your pump does not discharge water vertically, attach an elbow fitting to send the stream of water skyward so it rises above the water surface. A valve may be used to adjust the height of the spray. Use a diverter valve to allow water from the pump to go elsewhere if the pump powers other features. Even if you intend to operate just one fountainhead with the pump, a diverter valve will allow you to fine-tune the spray pattern easily. This frees the pump for a second purpose in the future, assuming the pump is strong enough.

LIFT PROPERLY

When a pump is attached to a fountainhead, you'll damage the pump if you try to lift it by the fountainhead. Disconnect the fountainhead from the pump before you attempt to lift it.

Choose from a variety of fountain types to add movement and sound to your feature. Consider the effects of a fine spray, a slow bubbling, or a gushing plume of water.

feature. If you use a solar pump to power the fountain, keep in mind that it will function only when the sun shines. Night, as well as shadows from visitors, clouds, and trees, will also prevent the pump from working.

Reinforce an Asian theme by recirculating water through a bamboo and stone fountain at the head of a small stream.

Affix the fountainhead to the pipe or diverter valve. Set the fountain jets and the decorative parts (if any) above the water's surface. If the setup wobbles, steady it with clean clay bricks stacked against the piping.

Keep water lilies and other aquatic plants in mind when planning a fountain. Rippling water from a vigorous fountainhead may retard or even kill water lilies and other aquatics. The spray patterns of some fountainheads, such as a multitier spray, make waves; others, such as the mushroom or bell fountainhead, return the water gently in a thin, transparent stream with virtually no surface disturbance.

The fine jets of fountainheads clog very easily and the fountain's spray symmetry may be lost. Prevent clogging by installing a mechanical filter that removes particles before they enter the pump. Alternatively, use a foam pump protector or a foam pre-filter, and clean it whenever you notice any lessening of water flow.

Enjoy the pleasure of a fountain even if you don't have electrical power available for your water

Bell or mushroom

Fleur-de-lis

Bubbler

Fountain kits offer a variety of fittings and spray heads to connect with your pump.

Rotating jet

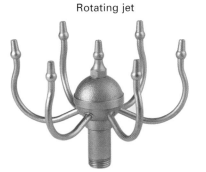

DECORATIVE FEATURES
continued

PIPED STATUARY

Although concrete piped statuary is popular, you may choose from other materials, including metal, plastic, fiberglass, and lightweight resin. Purchase a ready-made pedestal for your statue, or make a firm platform out of bricks or weathered concrete blocks. Place the statuary where it will spout into the water feature without spilling over the edge onto the ground. Setting the statue within the perimeter of the water feature eliminates the risk of water loss if a leak occurs.

Use flexible tubing to connect the statuary to its submersible pump and clamp the tubing securely at each end. If the pump discharge has a diameter different from the piping in the statue, buy fittings to make the transition complete. Small statuary, less than 12 inches tall, usually operates with a 125-gph pump;

Use a bridge to span a stream or waterfall and make an attractive vantage point for admiring the plants and fish below.

larger statues, more than 100 pounds and 24 inches tall, may require a 250-gph pump for optimal function. Enlist help to move large pieces of statuary to avoid the risk of injury to yourself and damage to the statue.

New, unweathered concrete statuary, as well as concrete blocks used to support statuary, require treatment before they're placed in a fishpond because the concrete can cause an unhealthy rise in the water's pH. Prevent problems by scrubbing the concrete with a stiff brush and a mixture of one part vinegar to two parts water. Rinse thoroughly and repeat two more times. Monitor the pond's water daily. If its pH exceeds 8.0, add a pH-lowering treatment according to the label directions.

BRIDGES AND STEPPING-STONES

A bridge or stepping-stones add a structural element to a water feature and invite you to step into the heart of it. You walk over the water to enjoy an otherwise unavailable perspective. When fish take to the shade of a bridge on hot summer days, you'll enjoy feeding them from that vantage point. As with any landscape feature, it's important to plan these structures in proportion to the surroundings. Locate them where they'll look natural and function practically. Choose building materials and styles for your bridge or stepping-stones that blend with the rest of the water feature.

Plan the design and plot the placement of a bridge or stepping-stones when you design your stream, bog, or pool. The weight of pounding foot traffic on these features makes a footing (foundation) necessary for them. Footings stabilize each stepping stone and each end of a bridge.

Most homeowners wanting a bridge buy a premade one or a kit ready for assembly. A bridge usually crosses a stream, pond, or other feature where the distance across the water is shortest. Select a bridge that will readily span this distance. Choose a formal or informal bridge style, according to your overall landscape plan. Although most bridges are made of wood, you may find a ready-to-install fiberglass structure.

BUILDING A BRIDGE

Anyone handy with carpentry tools can construct a basic wooden bridge that sits a few inches above shallow water. If the bridge is placed a foot or so above the water level, safety calls for a handrail. Practicality suggests making the bridge at least 3 feet wide to provide a comfortable space for two people to walk side by side.

A small garden pool becomes accessible and easy to cross with the addition of stepping-stones. The stones are set high enough to keep them from being perpetually wet and slippery.

Measure and stake the location for four concrete footings on which to rest the two bridge beams (8-foot-long 4×6s). Make four footing holes 6 inches deeper than the frost line in your region. Use a carpenter's level to make sure that all four footings have the same elevation. Half-fill the holes with gravel, then pour concrete to an inch or two above grade and recheck that all four footings are at the same elevation. Nail decking planks (2-foot-long 2×4s) to the beams, leaving ¼ inch between planks to allow rain to run through. Place the completed bridge deck on the four footings.

INSTALLING STEPPING-STONES

Large, flat rocks or concrete pavers make good stepping-stones. Use them to cross a narrow, shallow stream or the narrow part of a pond, or to lead toward the center of a pond where you might stand to get a closer look at the water lilies or to feed the fish.

Keeping safety in mind, locate stepping-stones away from a fountain or a waterfall, where the water's spray could make them slippery. Space steppers evenly, the width of a comfortable stride apart. For best results, use steppers at least 18×18 inches.

If you plan to use wood stepping-stones, use rot-resistant wood that doesn't contain toxic preservatives. Woods treated with creosote or pentachlorophenol or arsenic (CCA-treated)

kill fish. Because soft wood rots in water and requires replacement after a couple of years, use slabs of cedar or aged redwood. These will last several years as stepping-stones in water.

STEPPING-STONE FOUNDATIONS

Construct platforms of poured concrete to stabilize large stone steppers. Build a pier-type platform for more formal concrete steppers by mortaring concrete blocks or bricks into a stable base no more than 2 feet tall. If the water is sufficiently shallow that the stepping stones don't need a platform to rise above the water surface, place at least two layers of scrap liner, geotextile fabric, or old carpet under the stones to protect the liner (either flexible or rigid). Do the same when building pier-type foundations.

A FOUNTAIN EFFECT WITHOUT A FOUNTAIN

If you'd like a bubbly fountain effect without buying and installing a fountain, place the discharge pipe of your submersible pump an inch or so below the water's surface. Adjust the discharge closer to the surface for a higher, livelier effect; lower it for more subdued results. The higher the water goes, the more oxygenated it becomes. Fish benefit from the aeration. Remember this if your fish gasp for air, especially on a hot, muggy day when the oxygen level is at its lowest.

WATER TREATMENTS

Plants and animals thrive in a properly stocked pond. Aquatic plants and unseen beneficial bacteria represent living equipment that makes a healthy environment for fish.

Think of water treatments as you would regard prescription drugs. Avoid them if possible, but when necessary, use them as directed. Use only treatments designed for water gardens if you raise aquatic plants, ornamental fish, scavengers, and unseen-yet-beneficial nitrifying bacteria. Algae control treatments and water test kits for swimming pools work well in swimming pools, but the treatments kill all water garden life and the pool test kits aren't designed to show what a pond keeper needs to know.

CHLORINE AND CHLORAMINE REMOVAL

Public water departments routinely use chlorine or chloramine (chlorine combined with ammonia) to treat water. Both chemicals kill fish. Chlorine and chloramine removal treatments work almost instantly. Follow label instructions. Chlorine naturally escapes when exposed to the atmosphere, making pond water fish-safe two to three days after the water is drawn. If adding less than 10 percent to the volume of water already in the pond, there is no need to dechlorinate. However, if adding more than 10 percent to the volume of water in the pond, add dechlorination treatment to neutralize the chlorine.

Chloramine, a powerful antibacterial agent, remains in water for months, making treatment mandatory if fish are to survive. Add chloramine treatment (which also removes chlorine) each time you add chloramine-laden water to top off the pond. If you add about 5 percent of the water volume, treat the pond with 5 percent of the quantity needed to treat the entire pond. Check with your public water department to learn what is used to treat public water; rarely do water officials make a public announcement when switching chemical additives. Chloramine shows up on the ammonia test in the pond water test kit. Weekly monitoring for ammonia could save your fish.

Fishkeepers who use public water need to maintain a sufficient supply of antichlorine or antichloramine treatment for a complete water change. Discovery of toxic matter in the water, a massive leak, or an accidental overflow of water call for the immediate use of these water quality treatments.

ALGAE CONTROL

Avoid using algaecides in your pond. They contain chemicals toxic to fish and plants.

Flocculating clarifiers are designed to eliminate cloudy water created by algae and dirt. These products cause suspended material, including algae, to clump together and fall to

WHEN APPLYING ALGAE CONTROL

When you use an algae-control agent, your pond water loses oxygen as it is absorbed by the killed, decaying algae. The decaying algae may consume so much oxygen that the fish become stressed or possibly suffocate. Monitor fish for signs of stress, such as gasping at the surface or listlessness. Aerating the water with a waterfall, a fountain, air stones, or water sprayed through the air from a garden hose into the pond makes up for the oxygen depletion. Be especially alert to this potential situation when the water temperature is over 80° F. As the temperature rises, water holds less oxygen, while fish consume more oxygen.

the bottom of the water feature, where it decays. Lighter-weight particles float and mechanical filtration, vacuuming, and skimming easily remove the heavier particles. Results of this treatment show quickly, often within 24 hours. Dense algae growth requires an additional treatment or two, spaced one week apart. Potent for only a day, the liquid clarifier destroys only algae growing on the day of application. Apply it again when algae reappear.

Private water gardeners sometimes imitate the botanical garden technique of using black dye that gives the water a mirrorlike reflective quality. Black dye sets off the aquatic flowers and foliage. It also makes the water seem deeper, highly reflective, and clean. Nontoxic to fish, plants, nitrifying bacteria, pets, wildlife, and people, the dye costs little. Some pond keepers prefer blue dye. Either dye provides protection for fish from birds of prey, yet the owner sees the fish clearly as they surface to eat. Fish remain visible to a depth of 8 to 15 inches, depending on the amount of dye used. If the water is too dark, it may slow plant growth. Use dye sparingly at first, then increase the intensity accordingly.

Barley straw placed in a pond or stream seems to prevent algae growth when introduced in the spring ahead of such growth. Scientists are researching why, but the generally accepted theory is that straw, especially barley straw, releases a substance that prevents algae from reproducing. Its effect on established algae seems minimal, but it does appear to block reproduction. Most water garden suppliers carry barley straw.

BENEFICIAL BACTERIA

By now you know that beneficial nitrifying bacteria remove ammonia and nitrite from the water. They colonize around whatever surface areas they find in the pond. To get their work off to a good start, add concentrated bacteria to the biological filter and around the pond itself. These bacteria are sold in dry and liquid forms. The liquid form acts more quickly but has a shorter shelf life and costs more. You can confirm that the bacteria in liquid form are alive by their strong barnyard odor. Once in the pond or biofilter, they produce no noticeable odor.

WATER-QUALITY TEST KITS: LIFE AND DEATH

When water quality fails to meet fish requirements, the fish die. Test kits enable you to check pond water to tell if it has unsafe levels of certain chemicals. When ammonia and nitrate reach toxic levels,

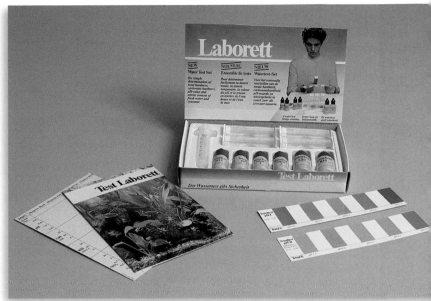

A water-quality test kit can signal early warning of a problem, giving you time to take corrective action and prevent a fish catastrophe. Use the kit daily at first and then weekly.

for instance, fish become listless, uninterested in eating, and more subject to disease and parasite attack. Chlorine and chloramines must be absent. Ammonia and nitrite levels must be low. The preferred pH reading is between 6.8 and 8.0. Stress becomes a threat if pH is under 6.5 or over 8.5. As pH increases, ammonia becomes much more potent and more likely to kill fish. Check the readings daily in midmorning when establishing a fishpond.

Most test kits don't enable you to test for the level of dissolved oxygen in the water. If oxygen is low, however, the fish tell you by gasping at the surface. Other water-quality deficiencies may also cause them to gasp. Once you become comfortable with the daily readings from a water-quality test kit, weekly checks will suffice. Also, as you get to know behavior patterns of the fish, you'll be able to read their signs too.

Test kits work by having you add an agent to a pond water sample or dip treated paper strips into pond water, then matching the resulting color with a chart.

OLD-FASHIONED TREATMENT STILL WORKS

Add a pound of sea or solar (noniodized) salt per 100 gallons of pond water as a tonic for lethargic fish. Gradually introduce the salt over two to four days. This treatment stresses algae, pathogenic bacteria, and parasites. Use the salt treatment only once, because the salt remains in the pond until the water is drained. Salt does not vanish with evaporation.

MAINTENANCE EQUIPMENT

Fishnets and leaf skimmers have telescoping handles that extend your reach. Pond netting thwarts predators.

DEICER NOTES

Operating a pump or air stones (an aeration device that releases air bubbles through the water) when using a deicer causes currents that move the warmed water away from the deicer, making it consume extra amounts of power to warm colder water. In addition, deicers emit a small, harmless charge into the water that might trip the circuit breaker if it's connected to a sensitive GFCI. In this event consult an electrician to determine if the GFCI can be replaced with a less sensitive one.

Autumn leaves drifting on the water surface may look appealing, but they foul the water and threaten the health of your fish. A leaf skimmer is a flat, netlike device that you sweep across the water to collect fallen, floating leaves. Ideally, its handle reaches halfway across your pond. Some skimmers come with a handle; others need you to add one. The same handle (either fixed length or telescopic) that you buy separately for the skimmer usually works with a pond vacuum and a fishnet.

Fishnets typically are made of long-lasting nylon or cotton, which is softer and thus gentler for fish, with $\frac{1}{8}$- to $\frac{1}{16}$-inch openings. The fishnet should be at least as wide as the longest fish in your pond. A deep net gives you better control than a shallow one when catching fish.

NETTING FISH

Healthy fish easily evade most overt attempts to net them out of a pond. Experienced fishkeepers slowly maneuver the net under the fish as the fish eagerly eat floating fish food, catching them unaware. Koi keepers use a net to guide a fish into a plastic pan, then carry the fish in the pan to its next location. This procedure minimizes loss of the fish's protective body slime.

LEAF NETTING

A sheet of lightweight plastic leaf netting prevents pond pollution caused by fallen leaves. In autumn, before leaves begin falling, stretch leaf netting over the pond. Select netting with openings in the mesh that are small enough to catch most of the leaves that would fall into your pond. Support the net above the water using 2×4s or beach balls; secure edges with stakes or bricks. Deluxe netting kits include poles for creating a tent effect that allows leaves to roll off toward the pond edges.

POND VACUUMS

Pond vacuums suck up debris from the pond bottom. The simplest type consists of an empty cylinder on an extended handle. It works like a siphon as debris-laden bottom water replaces air in the cylinder. A garden hose powers the venturi-type vacuum. It collects debris in a fine-mesh bag attached to its sweep head. As with a home vacuum cleaner, you can change sweep heads; use a small one for fine debris or a large head to collect leaves. To remove debris covering the bottom of a drained pond, use a wet-dry shop vacuum.

POND DEICERS

A floating deicer maintains a hole in the ice that forms on a pond in cold-winter regions, allowing oxygen to reach the water and the toxic gases that arise from decaying material to escape. Both actions are vital to the well-being and survival of your plants and fish.

Basically, an electric deicer is a heating element attached to a float. It's plugged into a 120-volt outdoor outlet with a GFCI. The deicer's thermostat turns on the heating element as the water temperature approaches

PROTECTING NETS

For a longer-lasting leaf skimmer or fishnet, look for a protective covering over the rim of the net. Without this protection, the net will wear out quickly. When not in use, store the net away from the deteriorating effects of sunlight.

Although a frozen waterfall creates a spectacular winter garden scene, a power outage could freeze its water line.

A deicer can become a fish lifesaver if ice lingers for days on the pond's surface.

freezing and turns it off as the surface water temperature rises above freezing, heating a small volume of water in its vicinity. Most deicers are 1,000 or 1,500 watts, the equivalent of 10 or 15 lightbulbs of 100 watts. Hang a 50-watt deicer on the side of an in-ground container garden of 50 gallons or less.

NONELECTRIC ICE MELTER

This insulated floating device maintains an ice-free area using no electricity. Within a 12- × 12 × 8-inch styrene block, a metal tube allows slightly warmer lower water to rise to the pond's surface. A vented styrene cap keeps out freezing air while allowing air and gases to escape as the warm water rises.

DETERRING PREDATORS

Predators—both winged and four-legged varieties—can wreak havoc with their uninvited visits. Fish-eating birds, raccoons, and cats are the usual culprits. One solution: a barking dog that patrols the grounds. Alternatively, a properly installed low-voltage electric fence effectively guards against creatures such as raccoons. Connect the 12-volt fencing to a transformer that operates off 120-volt household current. If your water feature attracts prowlers at night, set the electric fencing on a timer that turns the

current off after sunrise to avoid shocking children and family pets.

Motion-detector systems that include an intermittent impulse water sprinkler may keep predators away. But predators may soon lose their fear of the surprise sprinkling while unsuspecting humans get wet. Scarecrows, imitation owls, imitation snakes, and the like also achieve initial success, typically followed by a return of the problem.

Designed to scare off predators, this motion detector is attached to a garden hose and adjusted to sense even small movements. It sprays intruders with a burst of water.

*Taking advantage of an existing grade, this
waterfall looks beautiful among the naturalistic
rock outcroppings. When designing a falls,
keep in mind that considerable quantities of
water can be lost if allowed to splash outside
the water channel.*

MAKING DESIGNS AND PLANS

Before grabbing a shovel, put your water feature vision on paper. The more thorough your plans, the more likely you'll realize the pool, bog, stream, or waterfall of your dreams.

Begin with an idea of what type of feature would integrate nicely into the existing landscape, suiting the style of your home as well as your outdoor living style. Do you seek a place for contemplation or a hub for family activities; a place to expand your gardening skills or a way to deal with a confined site? Would a low-maintenance waterfall fit your lifestyle better than a fishpond?

Consider how the water feature suits the region as well as your taste preferences. Would you prefer a pond-waterfall-stream combination that dominates the landscape and provides interest year-round? Would a sprawling pond surrounded by mounds of earth and a gushing waterfall appear out of place where the natural terrain is flat?

Next, think about the size of the feature. Keep the scale of the project in proportion to its surroundings. One of the most common mistakes is building a water feature that is too small. Make the feature as big as your landscape and budget allow. Or if your site is small, you might prefer a quiet pond and stream tucked into a secret part of the garden. Create the illusion of space by building a long, narrow pool or by planting trees and shrubs on the far side of the pond.

Careful planning pays—literally. An improperly installed feature doubles or triples the effort and expense needed to correct it. Good planning requires doing your homework: Research the design and construction in books and magazines and on videos and websites. Go on local pond tours and interview pond-building professionals to gather helpful advice that could save you money in the long run.

As you select a site and design your water feature, consider how your plans will be affected by other elements, including sunlight, proximity to living space, year-round views, trees, drainage, and utilities. Then map out a site plan on paper. The basic site plan should include property lines; the house and other structures; trees, shrubs, and planting areas; utility cables (overhead and underground); sun-shade patterns; and prevailing winds. Look at the plans for water features on the pages ahead and gather information and inspiration for your design.

Finally, devise a construction plan that indicates the scope of your vision. The plan should include the materials, equipment, tools, aquatic life, and plants you'll need to bring your dream to life. Include a calendar to help you organize. It could begin with dates for choosing and excavating a site, purchasing materials, installing water and electrical supplies, and so on. A construction plan also helps you decide if and when you'll need professional help or other assistance with the project. Estimate which parts of the process you could accomplish in a day or a weekend. For example, excavation might take you several days or more with a shovel; a pro could do it in a fraction of a day with a backhoe.

Long stone slabs and a stone lantern are traditional elements in this Japanese-inspired stream. The clean lines and quiet trickle of water create a serene setting.

SITING THE WATER FEATURE

How do you determine where to locate your water feature? It's not as simple as building a pond in the largest open space your yard provides. You must consider a number of factors, all relevant to the design process, and each affecting the success of your finished project.

In the process, consider as many different scenarios as possible. Apply each of the following site elements to the locations: In some regions, for instance, a cool, shady location on the north side of a house would be slow to warm up in spring and take the brunt of active winter winds. This wouldn't be a good spot for a pond with fish and plants, but it could be right for a stream or waterfall.

1–SUNLIGHT

Think about how much sun and shade the site receives and how this will affect your water feature. Most blooming plants require at least six hours of direct sunlight each day. Yet the partial shade and windbreak created by trees, shrubs, or a building benefit plants and fish, especially during the hottest times of the day and year; it helps to slow evaporation too. Small and aboveground ponds, which heat up more rapidly than large, in-ground ponds, benefit most from partial shade. A shady site might suit a formal pond with few, if any, plants.

2–PROXIMITY TO LIVING SPACE

Locate a water feature where it can be viewed from several rooms inside your house as well as from a porch, deck, or patio, to ensure its year-round enjoyment.

Consider convenience: The easier it is to reach the water feature from your house and other locations, the easier maintenance will be. Building your retreat near traffic or a neighbor's fence could detract from its

Create a compelling view from indoors as well as outdoors when you add an inviting water feature to the landscape. This backyard paradise has more to offer than sparse turf.

relaxing qualities. Stand on the proposed site of your water feature and look away from the site from different directions. You may discover limitations that you hadn't noticed before, or you may discern just the right spot for a bench, a dock, or a bermed planting bed.

3–SEASONAL VIEWS

Imagine how the waterfall, pool, or stream will look in each season. Could you see the feature from the house if weather keeps you indoors? Will it be hidden from view when the trees are in leaf? Is the stream so shallow that the water will evaporate in hot weather?

4–TREES

Although trees provide outstanding and valuable elements in a landscape, they pose challenges to siting a water feature. When their leaves or needles and other debris fall into the water and decompose, water quality begins to decline. Over time, the polluting effects of decaying organic matter threaten or even kill fish in a pond and make the water murky. In addition, the shade under trees may be so heavy it prevents plants from flourishing in and around the water feature.

Trees, however, provide needed shade as well as a windbreak; they help prevent the swings in water temperature that stress plants and fish. Plant trees away from the feature— at a distance of up to 10 times the mature height of the trees or shrubs. Select a species that drops its leaves at once rather than all year long. Then, you can stretch netting to catch falling leaves.

Beware of locating a water feature within range of tree roots that could interfere with construction or damage the feature's structure and cause costly repairs. Building over its roots may also injure or kill a tree.

5–STORM DRAINAGE

Avoid locating your feature in a low-lying area where it could capture runoff from heavy rains or, worse yet, fill with a muddy washout. A major problem arises if storm water seeps under a pond and lifts it out of its excavation. In addition, toxic chemicals from lawn runoff threaten the ecological health of a water feature. If you have a low-lying site, consider filling it partially before building an aboveground feature on it. Building on a sloping site also presents challenges from heavy rains or runoff. A stream or waterfall, or a terrace topped with an aboveground pond, could be just right in this situation.

6–UTILITIES

Avoid locating your water feature over electrical, water, sewer, or gas lines. Also, consider how you'll get water and electricity to the feature. The closer the feature is located to existing electricity, the less expensive it will be to run a line to it. As long as you can reach the feature to top off the water level with a garden hose, you won't need to install a water line to it.

WATER FEATURES AND CHILD SAFETY

A water feature raises safety concerns, particularly when young children live near it. Plan ahead and provide for safety by following these suggestions:

■ Never leave children unsupervised near water.

■ If you have a toddler in your family, you might want to delay construction of the water feature. Meanwhile, make a large sandbox and convert it later into a pond or bog garden.

■ As other alternatives to a pond, consider building a fountain bubbling over stones or a dry creek that will carry water only during wet periods.

■ Locate the feature within easy view of the house and the yard.

■ Put a fence around your water feature or your property to keep neighborhood children from wandering onto the site. Your insurance coverage may require a fence with a childproof gate.

■ Consider building a raised or partially raised pond that affords a measure of security.

■ Lay a safety grate over a pond that allows plants to grow through it but rests securely a few inches below the water's surface. Black or blue dye in the water will disguise the grate.

■ For added safety, install a motion-sensitive alarm when you construct the feature.

■ Ask local authorities about requirements for safety, permits, and inspection.

DESIGN PARAMETERS

Huge rocks or boulders make a water feature more spectacular but require professional expertise to put in place.

The design of your water feature should meet your interests, suit your site and budget, and provide a healthy environment for plants and fish. Beyond these overall goals, you'll need to address specific parameters. Plan for views from inside the house as well as around the yard; and keep safety in mind as you plan.

A detailed site plan proves vital to a successful project, whether or not you do the construction yourself. The plan—a scale drawing sketched by you or rendered by a professional—helps you throughout the process of building a water feature, from generating design ideas to obtaining building permits and buying the right amount of material. An easy way to make a site map begins with the plat, or legal map, from your county assessor's office that shows the exact size and shape of your property. It usually includes fixed structures, such as the house, driveway, and fences, and their measurements. Make copies of the master plan and use them to sketch variations. Measure the area of the proposed pond. Use stakes and string, a rope, or a hose to outline the pond. Allow yourself to create several schemes at this point.

Use the following list to help you plan all the other details for your water feature.

SIZE: No area is too small or too large for a pond, but the space and feature should complement each other. A too-small pond looks like a stain on the lawn; too-large ponds dwarf the surroundings. Although starter ponds are inexpensive and easy to install, they're not easily kept in balance and quickly become a source of frustration. Remember the common remorse of pond owners: "I should have built it bigger."

SHAPE: Sketch the pond's shape within its surroundings. A symmetrical shape fits a formal setting; an irregular shape may complement the nearby landscape so well that it looks as though it has always been there. If you use a flexible liner, the size and design of your feature are unlimited, but a simple design reduces the likelihood of wasted flexible liner and minimizes installation challenges.

COMPONENTS: First decide if you'll build a water garden, a fishpond, or another feature. A koi pond benefits from being connected to a lily pond or bog. Plan any linking ponds, a stream, or a waterfall. Consider a raised pond for added child safety or extra seating, or to avoid digging in rocky terrain. Visualize an added fountain, bridge, or other special feature.

DEPTH: Plants and fish will have enough water to be healthy if the pond ranges from 18 to 24 inches deep. This depth minimizes water temperature variance, algae growth, and overwintering problems in areas as cold as Hardiness Zone 3. Make koi ponds between 3 and 6 feet deep.

DRAINAGE: Plan for drainage inside as well as outside your water feature. Include a bottom drain or perhaps a bulkhead connection for a koi pond (but not usually for other water features). A sloping site may require a retaining wall or uphill drainage. Examine the terrain to determine if storm water will flow naturally off the property or toward an in-ground drain.

ELECTRICITY: Plan for 120-volt, 20-amp power to your water feature, including a GFCI and PVC conduit. The power outlet should be set back from the water's edge at least 6 feet, or more if local regulations require.

WATER: Use a garden hose from the nearest faucet to fill the water feature. Only elaborate features need a separate water line.

ACCESS: Plan easy access to the feature from at least two directions, allowing for ease of maintenance and viewing. Provide a stable edge that is sturdy enough for you or visitors to stand on it. Build a reinforced-concrete collar under the pond edging; mortar flat, heavy stones over the liner edge to increase stability.

EDGING: Design edging to overhang the pond at least 2 inches to conceal the liner and discourage fish from jumping out of the pond. A slightly raised edge prevents surface water from entering the pond.

SHELVES: Shallow shelves permit pond water to warm faster; they are of benefit to ponds in areas with cool summers and mild winters. But in areas with hot summers and cold winters, shelves allow the water to heat up in summer, to the detriment of fish, and they make a smaller area for fish to hibernate over winter. Shelves also increase the likelihood that uninvited predators will knock over shallow-water containers. Omitting shelves reduces temperature fluctuation and provides flexibility to change plantings at will. Whether or not shelves are included, design one or more areas of the pond for marginal plants. The addition of shelves neither increases nor decreases the number of square feet of liner material needed.

LANDSCAPING: Integrate the water feature with the site, using planting areas, a meandering path, a beach, decking, or a sitting area. Dig a 1-foot-deep test hole in the proposed site to make sure the area is free of tree roots and the subsoil is not rocky or otherwise impenetrable.

EQUIPMENT: Estimate your needs for a pump and filter system, along with accessories. In general, think big and plan for contingencies. You may want to add a component to a pond later so start with the biggest pump and power supply you can imagine using. A koi pond works best when designed with a bottom drain, biological filtration, and a plant filter or adjacent water garden.

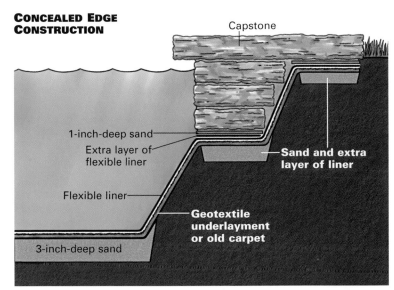

CONCEALED EDGE CONSTRUCTION

A pond design that includes a rock edge effectively conceals the liner.

Water seeps through the stacked-stone edge of a pond that features an adjacent bog where moisture-loving plants thrive in the saturated soil.

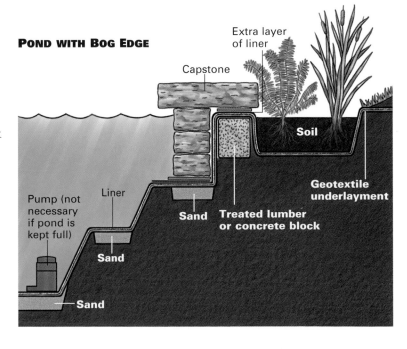

POND WITH BOG EDGE

DESIGNING A WATERFALL

A waterfall—serenely splashing or crashing—adds a captivating and exciting element to the landscape. The sight and sound will refresh and enchant you.

Large waterfalls at public parks and botanical gardens inspire smaller designs suitable for a residential property. Visitors to your waterfall will become fascinated as they gaze and listen.

When the delightful music of water cascades down rocks and into a pool, it attracts viewers before they can see the falls. Many homeowners have discovered that such an attractive feature masks nearby traffic noise.

Before planning a waterfall, look for inspiration. Take time to observe some of nature's creations. Notice the water basin or area at the top of the falls, how the water spills over and around the rocks, and how far it falls. Also, look at the land around the top, sides, and bottom of a fall. Visit private or public gardens that have waterfalls, including synthetic ones. Look at photos and artists' renditions of waterfalls. Ask landscape architects or designers to show you waterfalls that they have completed.

STYLE AND SUBSTANCE

Once you've gathered ideas, incorporate some into your plans and note others to avoid. The style of your waterfall should be obvious now. A formal design might include geometric elements, such as a straight-sided canal, stair-stepped falls, or a wall that water slides over. Popular building materials for formal designs include cut stone, tile, metal, and acrylic. The landscape could include ground covers or tailored trees and shrubs.

An informal or naturalistic design typically includes a single spillway surrounded by an outcropping of rocks or a rock garden. Or you might opt for a multiple-cataract waterfall, where more than one stream flows over the spillway. The plumbing for this design utilizes a manifold behind the falls that divides the water pipeline from the pump into two or more lines. Each line has its own valve to regulate how much water flows over each part of the waterfall and through the rock face as it discharges water between rocks at the top of the waterfall.

Watercourses consist of a series of basins or small pools linked by cascades or a tiered stream. As water overflows a pool, it either drops directly into a pond or spills onto rocks and into a stream. When two or more pools are connected by a waterfall or stream, design each lower basin of your watercourse larger than the one above it.

As the water recirculates in a watercourse, it is pumped from the lowest pond to fill the uppermost pool to overflowing. The lowest pond should be large enough that when water is pumped out of it to overflow the pool, the drop in volume won't be noticeable.

Final notes: If you design a pond with a waterfall, locate the falls on the far side of the main approach to the pond. Plan on a buffer of smooth rocks between a turbulent waterfall and the calm waters where water lilies grow.

BEGIN WITH THE SITE

Waterfalls look natural when built on a slope. If your property is level, create changes of level in order to make the water feature appear natural. When you excavate for the feature, save the soil and use it to sculpt berms, shape the watercourse, or create planting areas around the feature.

SIZE MATTERS

A 10 × 15 foot pool provides enough water to feed a waterfall about 2 feet high. It's possible to plan for five or six falls over several yards. Falls higher than 3 feet should be reserved for large ponds with extremely powerful pumps.

Limit your waterfall's height to 1 to 2 feet to keep it natural-looking and to limit water loss as it splashes outside of the waterway. Low falls also allow you to use a less-powerful pump to keep the water flowing. This not only saves money when buying a pump, it can result in substantial energy savings as the pump operates.

LINERS: FLEXIBLE OR PREFORMED

Like any water feature, a waterfall must be lined to prevent leakage. Choose from flexible liners and preformed plastic or fiberglass units, which come in a variety of sizes, shapes, and finishes. Preformed units come in several configurations, including pools, tiers, single cascades, and linking sections for a watercourse, allowing various arrangements. Flexible liners under the watercourse allow design flexibility.

ROCKS, ROCKS, AND MORE ROCKS

Choose rocks for your waterfall that are in scale with the pond. In natural settings, water courses over, around, and in between rocks. The water will break, splash, or tumble depending on how you arrange rocks above and below the edge of a falls or a stream. The placement of rocks not only builds the character of a naturalistic falls, but it also ensures its success. The size and shape of each rock affect the way water falls over it. Try several arrangements of rocks before hitting upon an ideal. Placed at the base of a falls, a large rock causes the water that strikes it to bubble and froth. Large waterfalls call for rockwork in scale with the water feature and the setting.

The flat rock over which water flows before falling is called the spillway rock. It should extend beyond the rocks below it. The farther it extends the greater the sound of falling water, because space behind falling water amplifies its music. The extension of a spillway also reduces or eliminates water weeping down the rockface of the waterfall.

DO YOU LIKE MOSS?

To encourage a mossy effect with green algae growing on your waterfall, keep the water flow slow, less than 50 gph per inch of sill. Discourage moss with 150 gph or more.

The piping scheme for a multi-cataract waterfall features separate pipes, each with an adjustable valve, that direct the water flow.

PIPE MANIFOLD BEHIND WATERFALL

Gate or ball valves

Flexible tubing

Rigid PVC pipe

DESIGNING A STREAM

A stream provides an aesthetic means of moving water from a plant filter to a water garden or koi pond.

A stream or watercourse typically runs from a waterfall to a pond. However, it can also function completely independently or be teamed up with another element, such as a bog garden. As with a waterfall, design the stream so it looks as though it had occurred naturally. Take as many clues from nature as possible. Check out rocky, gurgling streams in the hills or mountains, and slower, calmer, meandering meadow creeks. Observe how the water flows more quickly where a streambed narrows and slows in wider spots. See how rocks and other obstacles affect current speed and direction. Gather photos of areas that appeal to you. Naturalizing your watercourse with rocks and plants will be critical in making it look as though it belongs in your landscape.

WHERE TO BEGIN

If your property has a gentle, natural slope, it should lend itself well to stream construction. Let the stream follow the natural terrain if possible. Keep in mind that a stream is often more interesting if it is not all visible at once. Design the stream with an occasional dam so that it holds water when the pump isn't

operating. A vertical drop of 1 to 2 inches per 10 feet of length provides adequate flow. If the slope of your proposed stream area drops more steeply, create a series of long pools with vertical drops between them. This results in alternating runs and cascades (or waterfalls for more steeply sloping ground). The streambed needs to be approximately level across its width to look natural. If your site provides no natural slope, create one with the soil excavated to make the stream.

As with any water feature, begin your design with a site plan and sketches depicting the stream's placement and flow direction within your landscape. Curves and bends create a natural look—soft, flowing curves rather than quick, sharp turns. Water flows faster on the outside of a curve, and it pushes harder against the outside of the curve than its inside. Avoid long stretches of shallow water; algae will build up if the current is too leisurely.

Placement of natural rock determines the final appearance of the stream. Plan to acquire a variety of rock sizes and shapes. Use the larger stones to direct and channel water; use smaller pebbles to create a ripple effect as water flows over them. Placing rocks on the outside of the curve creates more turbulence there. Rocks may also be used to decrease the width of the stream, making water flow faster. They also enhance the visual effect, and in some cases add delightful sounds as water rushes by or over them.

STREAM LAYOUT

Use your site plan or a sketch as a guide to laying out the stream with a hose or rope. Think about where the piping will go. You'll want a straight, direct-as-possible pipeline from the bottom (source) of the watercourse to its upper end (head). The stream's source might be a waterfall, pond, or plant filter. Or water could appear to arise out of the ground like a spring flowing from a bed of rocks; the end of it is usually a sizeable pond. The water could disappear into a bed of rocks, disguising the housing for a pump that returns water to the stream head. However you design it, the catch basin should be large enough to hold all the water when the pump is shut off.

Consider adding bog gardens filled with marginal and bog plants adjacent to the stream. Bog gardens create natural transitions from the stream to surrounding dry-garden areas. Bogs look natural when positioned on the outside edges of bends in the stream, where they won't interfere with its flow.

DETERMINING THE PITCH FOR A STREAM

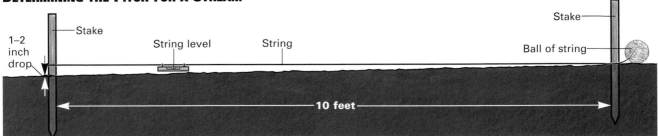

Stake

1–2 inch drop

String level

String

Stake

Ball of string

10 feet

The bogs receive water from the stream to replace whatever is lost through evaporation.

Your layout may lend itself to one or more vertical waterfalls, either along the course of the stream or at its end. The higher the vertical drop of water, the larger and deeper the pool under the falls should be. The greater area minimizes water loss from splashing.

Finally, design one or more places to cross the stream, depending on length and width. Options include bridges or stepping-stones.

WATER FLOW

Proper water flow ensures a stream's efficient function. The pump section of this book explains how pumps affect water flow. Construct the streambed first. Then use a garden hose to get a visual idea of how much flow is needed. Determine gallons per hour with a flow meter. Or find the gph flowing from your garden hose by filling a 5-gallon bucket using the hose. Divide 60 minutes by the number of minutes it takes your hose to fill the 5-gallon bucket. Multiply the quotient by five. After viewing the flow from your garden hose flowing through the stream, determine if you want more, less, or about the same gph for the stream. Purchase the pump that delivers the gph your stream needs.

When testing water flow, look for areas along the stream where water may overflow. Water containment is vital to avoid wasting water and constantly refilling the feature. If necessary, rework the sides so that the bank always keeps water within the stream. Consider aquatic plants you may want to grow in the stream as part of stream flow planning. A fast flow rate may discourage strong growth. Conversely, a too-slow rate leads to unsightly mats of algae. Striking a balance is critical to a beautiful stream.

One rule of thumb calls for the water to recirculate every hour or two—1,000 gph to 500 gph if your feature holds 1,000 gallons. Another rule to remember is that you need 1,500 gph per 12 inches of width at the sill of a waterfall or at the beginning of a stream.

The shallowness of streams encourages the growth of filamentous algae. Stream owners report that barley straw or barley straw extract, applied early and during the growing season, reduces or prevents this problem. Other points to keep in mind: Moving water, including cascades and waterfalls, stimulates additional evaporation compared to still water. Rocks in the stream sometimes trap debris, creating a dam effect that forces water over the stream bank.

Carefully placed rocks channel water as it flows from a stream into a pond, creating an attractive splashing effect.

ENLISTING PROFESSIONALS

The value of a professionally-rendered landscape plan will be evident in the completed, well-conceived project.

If you don't have the time or inclination to construct a water feature, consider hiring a contractor. The growing demand for water features has attracted the attention of landscapers and building contractors. Local home and garden shows present an excellent opportunity to meet water feature installers. Seek out those with whom you can easily discuss your project. Examine their portfolio of finished projects and ask for references. Visit several projects that have been in place at least two years. Remember, even though a feature's picture may exceed your expectations, arrange to inspect the feature in person to make sure that it functions properly. It is important to inspect contractors' work and talk with their clients.

A professional design helps incorporate a water garden into an outdoor living area, allowing you more time to enjoy the sights and sounds.

DEALING WITH CONTRACTORS

Get a written estimate of the project; be aware that the final cost may vary. Many landscapers offer to bill you based on hours of work plus materials and markup for overhead and profit. Request price quotes from several contractors. In some areas, specialized firms send a skilled team to install a complete water feature in a day. Verify that the contractor has a license (where applicable), insurance, and that all permits will be secured.

Agree on a final price, subject to completion of the project, and get a contract that details the terms. A contract price states the exact price agreed upon subject to a timetable as well as to completion of the project. If you make any changes from the agreed-upon specifications, be prepared to pay the contractor's asking price. If timely completion is critical, include a financial penalty if work is not finished within the agreed number of workdays. If a project takes weeks, provide partial payment as the work meets important defined points, holding back full payment until satisfactory completion of the project.

DESIGNS

Some contractors employ designers. For a modest fee, they create a plan in tune with your ideas. If you accept the plan, the design fee is applied to the overall price of the project. You can engage your own designer to make the detailed plan. Most designers work closely with landscapers and builders and can recommend contractors. Some designers will oversee the project for you. Large or complicated designs often work best when built by skilled professionals. However if you have experience as a do-it-yourselfer, you may find the plans on the following pages to be well within your abilities.

SIMPLE WATER GARDEN

FEATURES: A basic pond, adjustable to a large or small scheme that fits the site, this design provides an opportunity for diving into water gardening. This pond operates as a well-balanced system without either a pump or a filter. The plan represents an informal pool that combines plants and reflection. Add fish for more delights.

BUILDER'S NOTES: Easy to construct and maintain, this classic water garden with a winding path to the house provides outstanding views from indoors. The pond's mortared stone edging encourages access for maintenance and closer viewing.

APPROXIMATE SIZE: 10×15 feet
VARIATIONS: A wildlife pond, including a shallow beach and a variety of plants attractive to wildlife; a hidden garden, with mysterious appeal, that offers a quiet retreat in an enclosed, out-of-the-way spot. The path could be traded for a bermed area with a waterfall. Add a stream, an adjacent paved entertainment area, or a fountain. Alternative building materials: preformed liner; cut stone, concrete pavers,

or wood decking for edging; and endless variations of plants.
SUGGESTED EQUIPMENT: No special equipment needed.

MATERIALS

- 1 pond liner, rubber, 15×20 feet
- 1 geotextile underlayment
- 2 to 3 tons sand
- 5 bags mortar ready-mix
- 1 ton washed gravel
- 1½ tons river rock
- 3 potted water lilies
- 10 potted marginal plants, such as cattail, rush, cardinal flower, and papyrus
- 36 bunches submerged plants, such as anacharis and cabomba
- 20 black Japanese snails
- 6 goldfish

COST ESTIMATE*:
$1,500 to $2,000

*Approximate cost; prices vary from one region to another and with the quality of materials.

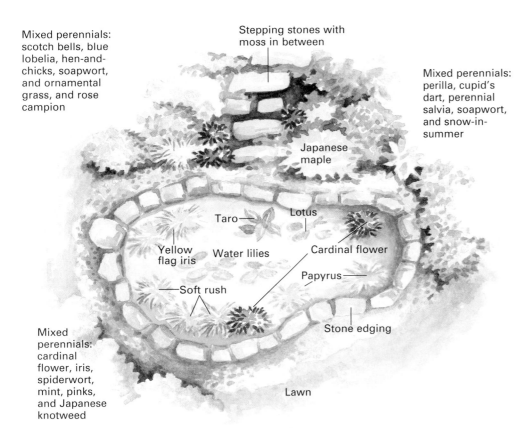

Mixed perennials: scotch bells, blue lobelia, hen-and-chicks, soapwort, and ornamental grass, and rose campion

Stepping stones with moss in between

Mixed perennials: perilla, cupid's dart, perennial salvia, soapwort, and snow-in-summer

Japanese maple

Taro — Lotus

Yellow flag iris Water lilies Cardinal flower

Papyrus

— Soft rush

Stone edging

Mixed perennials: cardinal flower, iris, spiderwort, mint, pinks, and Japanese knotweed

Lawn

PONDS WITH WATERFALL

FEATURES: A natural, gentle slope in the landscape makes an ideal setting for a watercourse. In this case, waterfalls link three stone-lined ponds. Careful planting around and among the rocks blends the watercourse with the landscape.

BUILDER'S NOTES: Perennials and upright evergreens surround the feature, linking it to the site and making it look natural. Large, flat stones provide spillways for the waterfalls and spots along the edge of the pools for sitting.

APPROXIMATE SIZE: About 20×50 feet overall (two pools 15×15 feet; one 20×20 feet)

VARIATIONS: The feature could include one, two, or three ponds with linking waterfalls, or a stream with cascading ponds. Make small or narrow bogs along the ponds. Extend the planting materials into the ponds, including water lilies and other aquatic plants. Add fish to the lower pond.

SUGGESTED EQUIPMENT:

- 2,000- to 4,000-gph submersible pump
- biological filter

MATERIALS

- 2 EPDM rubber liners, 20×20 feet
- 1 EPDM rubber liner, 25×25 feet
- geotextile
- 2 to 3 tons sand
- 40-pound bag gravel (for filling pots)
- 4 tons rock
- 55 feet PVC pipe or kink-free tubing
- fittings: L's, T's, and clamps
- black urethane foam
- 50 bunches submerged plants
- 50 black Japanese snails
- 8 comet goldfish
- yellow *Iris pseudacorus*

COST ESTIMATE:* $2,500 to $5,000

*Approximate cost; prices vary from one region to another and with the quality of materials.

Rose

Rose

Yellow flag iris

Mixed perennials and shrubs include sedum, lamb's-ear, chives, daylily, Japanese maple, creeping raspberry, ground cover juniper, blue fescue, yellow flag iris, and California poppy

Rose

Upright junipers

Upright junipers

RAISED POND WITH WATERFALL

FEATURES: This striking two-level pond, situated on a patio next to a Victorian-style home, takes a contemporary approach to the classical lines of a formal design. Besides providing the customary attraction of sparkling water, the waterfall with its music camouflages traffic noise and soothes the owners to sleep at night. Located in a frequently used area near the house, the raised pond provides hours of enjoyment while owners are dining or entertaining on the patio. The stone-capped walls provide seating and protect against an accidental plunge.

BUILDER'S NOTES: The centerpieces of the pond include a fountain and a waterfall. A 3-foot-wide sheet of water spills 18 inches into the lower pond and recirculates to the upper pool. The feature's stacked-fieldstone veneer and flagstone edging repeat building materials used to construct the nearby walls, steps, walkways, and patio. Plantings include water lilies, irises, and rushes. Statuary adds charm.

APPROXIMATE SIZE: 15×15 feet

VARIATIONS: Could be located at the edge of a deck; a different shape lined and edged with concrete; tile veneer or brick edging.

SUGGESTED EQUIPMENT:
- submersible pump for the waterfall
- submersible pump for the piped statuary
- 2 piped ornamental statuary pieces

MATERIALS

- 1 EPDM rubber liner, 20×20 feet
- 1 EPDM rubber liner, 10×15 feet
- 70 feet flagstone
- 3 tons fieldstone
- 5 hardy water lilies
- 15 irises
- 6 rushes
- 4 decorative stone or metal frogs
- 12 comet goldfish
- 50 bunches submerged plants
- 50 black Japanese snails

COST ESTIMATE:*
$12,000 to $18,000

*Approximate cost; prices vary from one region to another and with the quality of materials.

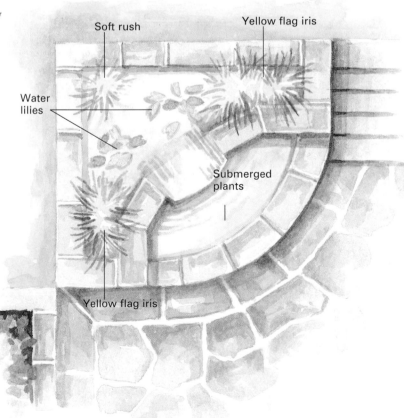

Soft rush

Yellow flag iris

Water lilies

Submerged plants

Yellow flag iris

STREAM

FEATURES: Two streams join to become one as they rush to two ponds below. A small waterfall connects the ponds; another small waterfall splits the stream in two. The rushing water draws attention to its beauty and sound. A strategically placed wooden bench invites the visitor to linger. The feature attracts wildlife and offers year-round interest. Landscaping includes trees, shrubs, and perennials suitable for shade.

BUILDER'S NOTES: Every stone is carefully selected and placed with consideration of how it would affect the water's flow. Excavating the 6-inch-deep stream takes one day; digging the double pond takes another day. Use an algaecide for a feature that doesn't include fish.

APPROXIMATE SIZE: Stream: 40 feet long and 18 inches wide; two pools 5×10 feet

VARIATIONS: Use a simpler design, including one pool and a single stream. Aquatic plants, such as iris and pickerel rush, could be added to quiet nooks in the stream. Water lilies, submerged plants, and marginal plants could inhabit the two ponds. Divert one-third of the water to run through a UV clarifier, enabling you to use a smaller pump and save money.

SUGGESTED EQUIPMENT: No special equipment needed.

Cedars of Lebanon

Atlantic blue cedar

Dwarf Hinoki cypress

Inkberries

'Sargentii' weeping hemlock

'Sunburst' St. Johnswort

Cotoneaster

Island planted with painted fern, Japanese maple, and hosta

'Karsten' Norway spruce

Japanese maple

Along the stream: umbrella pine, flowering dogwood, azalea, heavenly bamboo, sweet box, drooping leucothoe, and cotoneaster

MATERIALS

- 1 EPDM rubber liner, 5×45 feet
- 2 EPDM rubber liners, 10×15 feet
- geotextile underlayment
- 2 tons sand
- 1 ton washed gravel
- 2 tons river rock
- 4,000 gph pump
- 70 feet of 2-inch PVC pipe; 30 feet of 1½-inch PVC pipe
- fittings: one 2-inch PVC T-fitting; two 2-inch × 1½-inch PVC reducers; 2 gate valves; PVC elbows as needed; connector to pump (varies with pump)
- PVC glue
- UV clarifier (optional)

COST ESTIMATE*:
$3,500 to $5,000

*Approximate cost; prices vary from one region to another and with the quality of materials.

BOG

FEATURES: The bog garden duplicates nature's way of forming a transition between a wet area and dry land. This freestanding bog includes water-loving plants, known as marginals, that thrive in wet or moist soil. Exotic-looking plants add an element of the unexpected to the residential landscape. A bog provides an ideal opportunity to turn a poorly draining site into a beautiful asset.

BUILDER'S NOTES: Excavate to 16 inches deep; line the site with a 2-inch layer of sand topped with a flexible liner. Install a perforated pipe in the bottom of the bog, extending one end of it just above where the soil will be level so that you can connect it to a hose to keep the soil saturated. Cover the bottom of the bog with a 3-inch layer of gravel. Refill the bog with the soil saved from excavating; mix in generous amounts of peat moss.

APPROXIMATE SIZE: 10×15 feet

VARIATIONS: Make the bog a narrow strip, a small pocket adjacent to a pond or stream, or a sprawling wetland. Plant a bog garden in a large plastic tub sunk into the ground; fill it with a collection of carnivorous plants. Substitute leaky hose for PVC pipe.

SUGGESTED EQUIPMENT: No special equipment needed.

MATERIALS

- 1 EPDM rubber liner, 15×20 feet
- geotextile underlay (optional)
- 12 feet of 1½-inch PVC pipe
- elbow fitting
- hose fitting
- PVC sealant
- 1 ton sand
- 1 ton gravel
- rock for edging
- 1 bale peat moss
- immersible containers (optional)
- plants: *Salix lanata, Iris pseudacorus, Primula pulverulenta, Carex pendula, Lysichiton americanus, Onoclea sensibilis, Viburnum plicatum Mariesii,* and *Caltha palustris.*

COST ESTIMATE:* $550 to $800

**Approximate cost; prices vary from one region to another and with the quality of materials.*

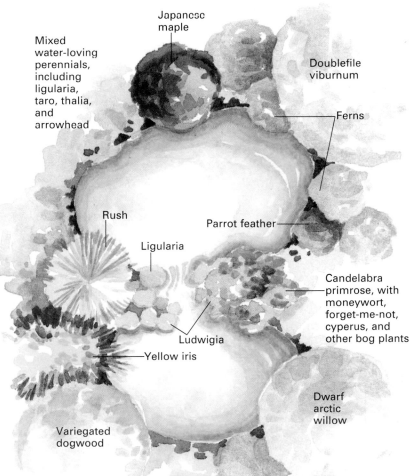

Mixed water-loving perennials, including ligularia, taro, thalia, and arrowhead

Japanese maple

Doublefile viburnum

Ferns

Parrot feather

Rush

Ligularia

Ludwigia

Candelabra primrose, with moneywort, forget-me-not, cyperus, and other bog plants

Yellow iris

Dwarf arctic willow

Variegated dogwood

Most often a pond makes an appropriate choice for a level site, whereas a waterfall suits a slope. Plan a low waterfall carefully to avoid an explosive volcano effect (left). Intersperse annual plants with rock edging to create a finished look that fills in and blooms quickly (below).

STEP-BY-STEP
CONSTRUCTION

In this section, we take you step-by-step through the construction of water features, bringing your designs and plans to reality. While the designing and planning translate your inspirations to paper, the construction results in the reality that you, your family, and friends will enjoy for years to come.

Preparation for construction is easier if you take into account the materials and equipment you'll need. Also, consider the effort needed to complete construction. Unless the project is small, have someone help with the work. Large projects may require equipment such as a backhoe. If so, you or a friend must be capable of operating one, or else hire an operator to do so. You may prefer to turn the entire project over to professionals.

The checklist below suggests factors to consider when preparing to build a water feature. Check with water-garden retailers and mail-order catalogs to figure prices.

The larger and more complex the feature, the more likely it is that you'll want professionals to do the job, especially if you are a first-timer. Using a professional increases costs. But having a guaranteed satisfactory feature relieves you of having to make troublesome corrections if a construction error causes problems. Correcting a faulty installation can take more time and effort than doing the initial construction correctly.

Coordinate your water feature construction with adjacent areas. Will it affect pathways, a patio, or deck? Will it affect your neighbors? Will shrubbery and trees be added nearby or taken away? Use this checklist below to avoid unexpected expenses.

WATER FEATURE CONSTRUCTION CHECKLIST

EXCAVATION
- ☐ Hand labor—shovel, pick, wheelbarrow
- ☐ Backhoe—hourly/daily rate, with or without operator. Check out delivery and pick-up charges.
- ☐ Disposal of soil—construct a berm if in flat area, regrade to suit, or haul away (rental truck?)
- ☐ Take into account the ease or difficulty of digging in the area. Sand, loam, clay, rock?

LINER
- ☐ Flexible liners (EPDM rubber, PVC, PVC-E, polyethylene)
- ☐ Rigid preformed liners (fiberglass, high-density polyethylene)
- ☐ Concrete—ready-mix, gunite, mortar

UNDERLAYMENT
- ☐ Sand
- ☐ Geotextile fabric
- ☐ Used carpeting
- ☐ Newspapers, cardboard (staple-free)

EDGING MATERIALS
- ☐ Stone, brick, or wood
- ☐ Gravel
- ☐ Boulders
- ☐ Foundation for boulders
- ☐ Machinery for setting heavy rockwork

MOVING WATER FEATURE MATERIALS
- ☐ Waterfall liner, sand, rocks
- ☐ Fountainheads
- ☐ Piped statuary
- ☐ Pump
- ☐ Pipe, tubing, fittings

WATER-QUALITY CONTROL
- ☐ Mechanical filter
- ☐ Biological filter
- ☐ Plant filter
- ☐ Bottom drain or bulkhead
- ☐ UV clarifier
- ☐ Pump
- ☐ Beneficial nitrifying bacteria
- ☐ Water dye
- ☐ Flocculating water clarifier
- ☐ Algaecides
- ☐ Barley straw

ELECTRICAL INSTALLATION
- ☐ Professional installation
- ☐ Materials

AQUATIC LIFE
- ☐ Plants
- ☐ Soil containers
- ☐ Soil
- ☐ Fertilizer
- ☐ Fish
- ☐ Scavengers

FISH AIDS
- ☐ Fish food
- ☐ Dechlorinator
- ☐ Water-quality test kit
- ☐ Thermometer
- ☐ Fishnet
- ☐ Deicer
- ☐ Pond netting
- ☐ Predator deterrent

MISCELLANEOUS
- ☐ Lighting
- ☐ Bridge
- ☐ Stepping-stones
- ☐ Automatic flow valve

CONSTRUCTING A POND WITH A FLEXIBLE LINER

Outline the shape of your planned pond on the ground to help you visualize how it will relate to existing features of the landscape.

Triangulation ensures right angles (90 degrees) when the distance between B and C is 5 feet; 4 feet between A and B; and 3 feet between A and C (or comparable proportions).

First, outline the pond's shape on the planned site. Use a garden hose or rope to outline a naturalistic, informal shape. Confirm the planned length and width using a measuring tape. Observe the layout over the next few days; modify it if you wish. When you're satisfied, use powdered limestone or flour to mark the final shape.

Marking the perimeter of a formal pond requires stakes and string to create straight lines, carefully measured angles, and perfect circles (*below left*). Make rectangles or squares using triangulation. Use a stake to mark the center of a circular pool. Attach the stake to a length of string equal to the radius of the circle. Walk around the stake with the string outstretched fully, marking the circular perimeter with flour or powdered limestone.

EXCAVATING THE SITE

A friend or hired help makes this laborious task easier. A professional pond installer comes equipped to deal with unforeseen obstructions that may lurk under the soil's surface. Or rent a backhoe if it's warranted by the size of the pond, its accessibility, and your ability to operate it efficiently.

Before you start digging, check with local utilities to ensure there are no buried cables. Be prepared with a variety of shovels, a pick, a digging bar, garden rakes, a soil tamp, and a wheelbarrow. If you plan to excavate an area of existing lawn, strip off the sod before you begin digging and removing any soil. Roll up the sod and save it in a shady place for use around the edge of the installed pond or elsewhere. Plan where you will move the excavated material. Some or all of the soil might be used to build a waterfall. If you have nowhere to put the soil, haul it away.

Determine the lowest point of the pond's perimeter. Unless part or all of the pond will be located above ground, this point defines the level for the top edge of the pond. Measure the pond depth from this point. Begin digging at the center and work out to the edges, being careful not to dig beyond the perimeter. Form the sidewalls carefully.

Excavate 8 to 10 inches deep where you plan to create a narrow shelf to support a stone veneer for hiding the pond liner; make it 6 to 12 inches wide (depending on the size of the stones used as veneer). Coping or edging will eventually rest on top of the stone veneer. The wider you make the shelf, the greater the loss of pond space. If you plan to use cement blocks to make sidewalls for the pool, excavate for the blocks. The depth of the excavation

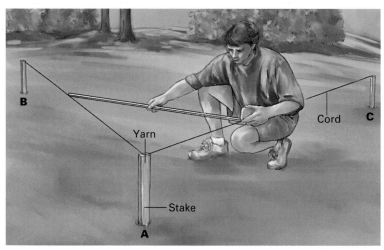

TRIANGULATION AND CIRCULAR LAYOUTS OF A POND

Take care to remove tree roots and rocks as you excavate the pond. Left in place they could damage the liner.

Successful pond construction requires that the top edge is level. Level the top edge of the pond using a board and spirit level.

depends on how deep the blocks will be set in the ground. Excavate 2 inches wider than the width of the blocks to allow room to work.

Ensure that the pond's top edge is level by laying a 2×4 across the excavation with the ends of the board on opposite sides of the pond. Set a spirit level on top of the board to confirm that the perimeter is level. Move the ends of the board around the perimeter to verify that the entire edge is level. For ponds too large for this method, use a central stake as a leveling reference. Extend a string to each point being checked, verifying the level each time with a spirit level. Survey equipment (available for rent in metropolitan areas) accurately confirms level using a theodolite or laser transit. Check depth and level as you continue to excavate. Allow yourself a margin of error plus or minus ¼ inch of level.

Form sidewalls with a slight pitch inward from top to bottom—a 10- to 15-degree slope works well for firm soil. Sandy soil works better with a 20- to 30-degree slope. Visually check the soil to ascertain whether it keeps the form you've excavated. If it lacks stability and glides down, make the slope less steep.

If the soil is not firm, tamp the edges. If you want steeper walls than the soil permits, consider forming the sides with cement blocks. Remove all rocks and tree roots from the sides and base. Fill any depressions with sand or soil.

If you live where summers are mild (few days above 80° F) or where winters are mild (few days with ice on the pond), you may include planting shelves. Excavate these as you shape the sidewalls. Planting shelves typically measure 10 to 12 inches wide and sit about 10 to 12 inches below the water's surface.

Make a small depression in the deepest area for future draining with a pump. The bottom should slope slightly, at the rate of 1 inch per 10 feet, toward the depression.

Lay a protective 2-inch base of sand on the pond bottom. Use the sand to fine-tune the gentle 1-inch slope per 10 feet. Next, install an underlayment of geotextile fabric, old carpet, or newspapers on the sidewalls and bottom.

Unlike most landscape projects, a water garden looks complete during its first season. In future seasons, surrounding plants grow over and around the rock edging, enhancing the waterscape as they soften its original starkness.

CONSTRUCTING A POND WITH A FLEXIBLE LINER
continued

Besides making the top edge of the pond level, you must be sure that the excavation measurements correspond with your plans. Avoid digging beyond what the liner can cover because replaced soil lacks the integrity of undisturbed soil.

INSTALLING THE LINER

Lay a protective 2-inch base of damp sand on the bottom of the pond. Use the sand base to fine-tune the gentle bottom slope. On the sidewalls, install an underlayment of geotextile fabric, newspapers, or old carpet. For extra protection, extend the underlayment to cover the sand bottom. Set preformed concrete pads in the bottom of the pond to support objects heavier than 200 pounds that will be placed in the pond, such as statuary, boulders, and bridge piers. Cover the concrete pads with carpeting

PATIENCE PAYS OFF

Wait five days before you trim any excess off your pond liner. Over this time, the weight of the water will cause the liner to give a little here and there as it settles into the excavation. Save some of the liner trimmings to use for repairing punctures or tears in the liner that may occur in years to come.

before installing the pond liner. Once the liner is installed, place three or four layers of scrap pond liner on top of the pond liner over the concrete pad. Lower the heavy object slowly and carefully onto the prepared area.

Upon completing the installation of the protective underlayment, carefully recheck the measurements of the excavation using a flexible measuring tape. Measure the length of the excavation by starting at the edge; lay the tape down the sidewall, across the bottom, and up the opposite sidewall to the edge. Add 2 feet to this measurement to determine the minimum length of the pond liner. On a line perpendicular to the length, measure the width. As with the length, begin measuring down the sidewall, across the bottom, and up the opposite sidewall. Add 2 feet to the measured width. Compare the measured results with the dimensions of the pond liner before opening the carton (you may need to exchange the liner for a different size). See page 11 for more details about measuring for a liner.

UNFOLDING THE POND LINER

With assistance, if needed, carry the liner into the excavation. Dragging could harm it and might pull damaging objects on top of the protective underlayment. Cold liners, especially those made of PVC, may require several hours in the sun to become pliable. Leaving it in place too long—such as for several days—could kill the grass.

Starting at the center of the pond, unfold the liner outward toward the sides. Center the liner over the excavation. Wear sneakers or go barefoot when walking on the liner to protect it. The liner will bunch up at curves and corners; folds are an inevitable result of forming a two-dimensional piece of material into a three-dimensional shape. Create a few large folds in order to eliminate most of the smaller ones. Let one person pull the liner from the top edge while another person works inside the excavation, making adjustments and ensuring that the liner remains centered in the excavation. Place smooth stones or bricks on the perimeter of the liner to prevent it from blowing into the pond.

Sneakers and soft-bottom shoes cause no damage to flexible pond liners. To fit a two-dimensional liner into a three-dimensional excavation, you must tuck and fold the liner.

TUCKING AND FOLDING

Informal pools will have random folds along the sides. Rectangular formal pools should have one large fold at each corner. Form each fold as a large triangle; secure it with double-sided seaming tape. Allow the seaming tape to cure for 24 hours (or as directed) before adding water. Sealing the fold not only makes it less obvious, but it also keeps out debris and prevents small fish from becoming trapped.

The time spent folding the pond liner should be minimal, less than 20 minutes for a 10×10-foot pool). Usually, the person most concerned about folds and tucks is the pond owner; few viewers ever take note of them. If debris falls into the lined pond, sweep the material into a plastic dustpan. When ready, fill the pond with 2 inches of water before making final adjustments to the liner by smoothing out some of the wrinkles. Finish filling the pond before edging it. After the pond is filled, check for low spots around the edge. If water doesn't cover the liner evenly to the top, or it spills over the edge in places, lift the liner and build up the soil in those places.

If care is exercised during the liner installation, no damage should occur. However, if you do puncture the liner, it is easily repaired with special adhesive tape designed for this purpose.

Place rocks to look natural. Stone dealers carry water-smoothed rocks that suit an aquatic setting; rocks blasted from a quarry tend to look artificial. When handling more than a few rocks, wear gloves.

INSTALLING A PREFORMED POND LINER

Choose the largest liner possible that suits your site and your pocketbook. Preformed units appear smaller once installed, filled with water, and edged. If you desire fish, the pond should be deep enough to accommodate them; if it has plant shelves, they should be wide enough to accommodate the containers.

After determining where you want to install your pond, carry the preformed unit to the site. Orient the liner, topside up, on the spot where you want to install it. Use a carpenter's level and plumb bob or a weighted string to establish the outer edge of the pond. You can't simply mark the outline of the form's bottom on the ground and start digging. Preformed rigid pond walls slope slightly inward (from top to bottom), making the top perimeter larger than the bottom perimeter. The plumb bob drops straight down from the top perimeter, enabling you to outline the perimeter on the ground directly below it. Mark the perimeter using a rope or

Before digging, place the prefabricated pool upright where it will be located, then map the outline using a garden hose or rope.

a hose. Enlarge the entire perimeter by 2 inches to allow working room within the excavation. The extra space will be filled later with sifted soil or sand. Finalize the outline by marking it with spray paint, flour, or sand.

EXCAVATING THE SITE

The liner must have firm support under the shelves, bottom, and sides in order to be stable and resist buckling. See page 64 for general excavation directions. Set aside the preformed pool while you excavate. If the pond has no shelves, dig straight down (or at a slight angle no greater than the inward slope of the preformed unit) to the bottom. The depth should match the depth of the pond form plus 2 inches. If the pond includes shelves, measure carefully to make the excavation conform to their depth and width. The shelves need to be supported by soil in order to sustain the weight of water when the pond is filled. Leave room to add 2 inches of damp sand under the shelves once the excavation is complete. Damp sand stays in place, whereas dry sand tends to shift off the edges of shelf areas during installation. If you want the top of the preformed liner to be 1 inch above ground level to protect the pond from surface runoff, then measure and dig out only 1 inch extra; the 2 inches of added sand will put the pond top 1 inch above ground level.

Avoid overdigging the shelf areas. Backfilling an excavated space under a shelf could cause the shelf to settle while the remainder of the pond remains stable. This would make the top uneven and allow water to overflow the edge around the shelf.

Decide in advance what to do with the soil removed during excavation. You may use it to build up an area planned for a waterfall or to change the contour of the land somewhere else on your property. Ask friends or neighbors if they need the soil. Otherwise, look for a place wanting clean fill dirt.

Use a spirit level to check that the sand-covered bottom and shelves of the excavation are completely level.

Comb the sand with a straight board to ensure that it is smooth.

PREPARING THE EXCAVATION

Spread 2 inches of damp sand across the bottom of the excavation on the shelf surfaces. Use a board or the straight edge of a garden rake to spread the sand evenly over the entire bottom and the shelves.

Place the liner into the excavation; use a spirit level to verify that the pond is level. If it needs leveling remove the preformed liner and rework the sand. The pond's contact marks on the sand indicate where to remove high sand and where fill-in sand is needed. Continue working the sand until the pond comes within ¼ inch of level. Add the edging.

Perhaps you plan to have a raised pond or one that is partially in the ground and partially above the ground. If it is to be partially in-ground, dig down as already described, but only far enough so that the top of the pond will be at the height desired. Remember to account for the 2 inches of sand added to the excavation. For an aboveground pond, remove the top 2 inches of soil and replace it with sand. Rake and work the sand as needed so that the top of the pond sits level.

BACKFILLING

Despite being made of rigid fiberglass and high-density polyethylene, preformed ponds have a bit of flexibility. Units built of these materials typically possess sufficient structural integrity to hold water without outside support. But because they are somewhat flexible, they may become distorted when filled if the sidewalls are not supported. Prevent the distortion by filling the space between the sidewalls and the excavation with sifted soil or sand as you fill the pond with water. Avoid using vacuum-formed pools, such as kiddie wading pools, because they easily change shape in undesirable and unpredictable ways, and they're difficult to install and maintain.

As the first few gallons of water spread evenly across the bottom of the liner, it's likely that the form will sit level in the ground, but the weight of added water might cause a slight shift. As the pond fills backfill around the form. Adjust the water flow so that the pond fills to roughly the same level

OUTLINING THE FORM

Easily outline the perimeter of the excavation, if your pond is symmetrically shaped, by turning the form upside down on the proposed site and spray-painting around its edges. This method works only for squares, rectangles, circles, and ovals but not for nonsymmetrical shapes.

at which you are working the soil on the outside of the liner. Periodically check the level in all directions three or more times while the pond is filling with water. If it's out of level by more than ¼ inch, remove the water and soil, make adjustments, and start over. Add the edging to complete the installation.

Lift the shell and lower it into the excavation. You may need to remove it several times to make adjustments.

Fill the unit with 4 inches of water. Begin backfilling around it with sand, tamping the sand as you work. Gradually add more water as you backfill, keeping the levels of sand and water comparable.

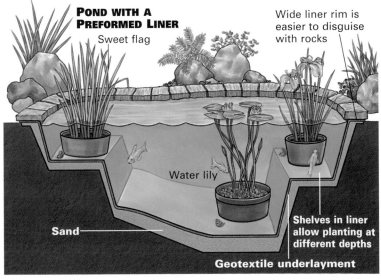

POND WITH A PREFORMED LINER
Sweet flag
Wide liner rim is easier to disguise with rocks
Water lily
Sand
Shelves in liner allow planting at different depths
Geotextile underlayment

CONSTRUCTING A CONCRETE POND

A pond made of concrete presents challenges for anyone inexperienced in building with this medium. In addition to digging an excavation, you must have carpentry skills for making the forms and masonry skills for pouring and finishing the concrete. If you lack experience, consider hiring a mason or a contractor with a proven record of successful pond construction.

Sturdy rebar makes any concrete water feature better able to withstand the damaging effects of seasonal freezing and thawing, as well as mild earth tremors.

Professional installers spray gunite on the excavation with rebar reinforcing in place. They quickly transform the hole into a recognizable pond for a water garden that will soon be in bloom.

For best results, the concrete portion of the job is completed within a day in a continuous process that leaves no seams.

GETTING STARTED

Begin with an excavation to a depth that allows for a concrete construction of a bottom at least 6 inches thick (4 inches in frost-free, earthquake-free areas) plus an additional 4 to 6 inches of gravel. The excavation must allow for walls equally as thick. Plan to allow the top of the concrete to extend 1 inch above the surrounding area to keep surface runoff out of the pond. If installing an irregular-shaped, natural-looking concrete pond, hire a contractor to apply gunite or other sprayed concrete to an excavation lined with reinforced wire mesh.

Otherwise, build wood forms that will shape the concrete into the desired design. Add the thickness of the wood-form walls and supports to the size of the excavation. The walls of the form must be put together carefully and neatly because the concrete walls will be an exact impression of the form. Make sure that the tops of the walls are level; the level of the pond cannot be altered once installed.

In cold areas where ice stays on the pond continuously for weeks at a time, consider making the walls 1 to 2 inches thicker at the bottom than at the top and angled slightly outward from bottom to top. The angle makes the walls better able to withstand the pressure of ice.

Build the forms with ¾-inch plywood held in place by vertical 2×4s spaced every 3 to 4 feet. At the top of the form, nail a horizontal 2×2×6-inch spacer between the boards to make the walls 6 inches thick (4 inches thick in warm regions).

THE POND BOTTOM

In areas subject to winter freezing, use ⅜-inch rebar wired together in a 12-inch grid, or a flexible wire mesh, to reinforce the bottom and walls. Add a 6-inch-deep layer of gravel to make a base that reduces the risk of settling and cracking, especially during the freeze-thaw cycles of winter or if the earth moves. Tamp it down.

When pouring the concrete for the pond bottom, make a saucer-like depression approximately 4 inches deep where you can place your pump when you want to empty the pond. The pond floor should slope toward the depression at the rate of 1 inch per 10 feet of bottom. This eliminates the need to install a drain (and prevents clogged drain problems) in the water garden. Ten years or more might pass before there is any need to drain the pond, although koi ponds usually include drains as part of the filter system.

POURING THE POND

For best results, pour the concrete in one day—ideally on a cool, cloudy day. If pouring during hot weather, cover the poured construction with opaque plastic sheeting to allow the concrete to cure slowly. Everything happens quickly once the concrete truck arrives. As soon as the ready-mix concrete leaves the mixer, it starts to set. The entire pond should be poured in a continuous process—first the floor, then the walls—to make a seamless form. This guards against the cracking that may occur where the poured areas join when one pouring partially sets before the adjacent pouring takes place. The pond floor should be carefully smoothed, beginning at one end and working backward toward the opposite end and maintaining the slight slope toward the center. Use a 2×4 laid flat to tamp the concrete in the form.

Apply optional concrete plaster to give the pond a smoother finish.

Lime from fresh concrete leaches into the water, raising the pH and posing a toxic hazard for fish and other wildlife. To alleviate this situation, fill the pond with water after the concrete sets, then drain it the following day. Using a stiff brush, scour the floor and walls of the pond with a mixture of 50 percent vinegar and water. Rinse thoroughly and refill the pond. Check the pH; stock fish when it remains in the safe zone (below 8.0) for at least 3 days. A 10 percent solution of muriatic acid works in place of the vinegar, but it has a strong unpleasant odor.

EXTRA SECURITY

It might take a decade or so, but concrete ponds eventually develop hairline cracks and begin to leak. Postpone the leaking by using a flexible pond liner around the exterior of a concrete pond. Lay a base for the liner with 2 inches of gravel topped with 2 inches of sand. Place an underlayment of old carpeting or geotextile fabric over the sand and install the flexible liner over that. Pour the concrete floor over the liner, then pour the walls. After removing the wall forms, wrap the excess liner and

underlayment over the exterior and top of the pond walls. Hold it in place on top of the walls using bricks or smooth rocks. Backfill the space between the underlayment and the excavation walls with sand or sifted soil. Cut off the extraneous liner and underlayment or fold them back to conceal them under the edging.

FINISHING

Add an edge, or coping, of brick, decorative tiles, rocks, or other material, to suit the site. Use mortar to secure the edging of your choice. You might elect to have a smooth concrete top for the pond walls. Apply a veneer of brick, tile, wood, or stone to the outside of an aboveground concrete pond if you wish.

CONCRETE ADVICE

Before excavating your site contact local concrete dealers to gather advice particular to your area. Climatic conditions, soil characteristics, earth movement, building codes, or other factors may require special modifications.

Completing the construction marks the end of one phase of the installation. For gardeners, the fun begins with the introduction of plants in and around the new pond. This pond was made deep enough to house koi.

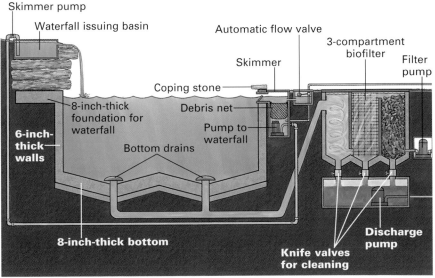

CONCRETE KOI POND

- Skimmer pump
- Waterfall issuing basin
- Automatic flow valve
- Skimmer
- 3-compartment biofilter
- Filter pump
- Coping stone
- 8-inch-thick foundation for waterfall
- Debris net
- 6-inch-thick walls
- Pump to waterfall
- Bottom drains
- 8-inch-thick bottom
- Knife valves for cleaning
- Discharge pump

CONSTRUCTING A BOG

Enjoy a rich variety of moisture-loving plants in a setting still rare in America—a planned, cultivated bog on a residential property.

Make a bog garden as an independent unit or as a part of one or more other water features—a pond, a stream, or a waterfall. The bog can absorb water that overflows from your water feature after heavy rains. And when you integrate a bog with other features, it takes little extra work to make it function as a plant filter that absorbs pollutants and silt.

In nature, streams and ponds have wet, boggy areas along their edges. In garden settings, a bog imitates a marshy place where plants grow in standing water or wet, spongy ground. Water-loving plants thrive because the soil doesn't dry out. Depending on the size and location of your bog, make a freestanding garden, as described here, or plant in the moist margins of a stream or pond, blending the boundaries of water and land.

Check with local environmental authorities before you do anything that would affect an existing wetland. State and federal laws protect wetlands, or places where moisture-loving plants, such as cattails, grow naturally.

MAKING A BOG

Bog garden construction differs from pond construction mainly in terms of depth. Excavate a bog 12 to 16 inches deep with sloping sides, saving the soil to refill the bog later. Spread a 2-inch layer of sand and top it with a preformed or flexible liner. Use geotextile fabric or a layer of carpet between the excavation and the liner. If the site remains moist naturally, skip the underlayment. Instead, perforate the bottom of the liner every 3 feet to allow slow drainage and prevent standing water from becoming foul.

To ensure that the bog never dries out, lay a perforated pipe in the bottom of the bog, leaving one end extending above ground at the side of the feature. Attach a fitting to the exposed pipe and connect it to a hose. Alternatively, connect it to a downspout to allow periodic flushing with rain water. Cover the bottom of the bog (and the pipe, if installed) with 3 inches of gravel. Fill the bog with soil saved from the excavation; add a wheelbarrow full of peat moss per 100 square feet, working it into the soil to improve its moisture-holding capacity.

Build a rim of soil and extend the bog's liner an inch above the surrounding ground to keep water from running off. Use rocks, soil, and plants around the perimeter to disguise the liner and give the bog a natural look.

PLANTING THE BOG

Many bog plants spread gregariously, quickly overrunning slower-growing species. Keep this in mind when you create a planting scheme, determine where to locate plants, and decide if you will plant in containers. Use plastic nursery pots or water garden baskets to contain invasive plants. Otherwise, plant directly in the soil. Saturate the soil, using a leaky hose laid on or under the soil surface or attaching a hose to the end of a pipe installed in the bog.

ADDING A BOG GARDEN

Build a bog adjacent to a lined pond or stream by extending the liner of the water feature into the bog excavation. The edge between the pond or stream and the bog must be semipermeable, meaning it will allow water to seep into the bog and saturate its soil. Where the two features meet, the soil should be bermed and hard-packed. After you extend the liner over this berm and into the bog, stack rocks, concrete blocks, or layers of sod soil side up on the bermed area. (Use another piece of flexible liner to cover the bog if the liner from the pond or stream won't cover it.) The rocks or sod will keep the bog's soil out of the pond but allow water seepage into the bog.

Left: *Cardinal flower* (Lobelia cardinalis) *thrives in moist soil and full sun, where it will reach up to 3 feet tall.*

Above: *A large bog construction includes placing a flexible liner on top of the excavation and topping it with several layers of stone and gravel.*

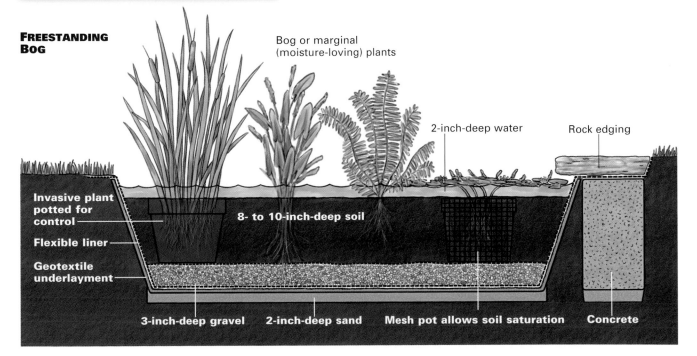

FREESTANDING BOG

Bog or marginal (moisture-loving) plants

2-inch-deep water

Rock edging

Invasive plant potted for control

8- to 10-inch-deep soil

Flexible liner

Geotextile underlayment

3-inch-deep gravel   2-inch-deep sand   Mesh pot allows soil saturation   Concrete

INSTALLING A PREFORMED WATERFALL

CROSS-SECTION OF INTERLOCKING ISSUING BASIN AND CASCADE WATERFALL UNIT

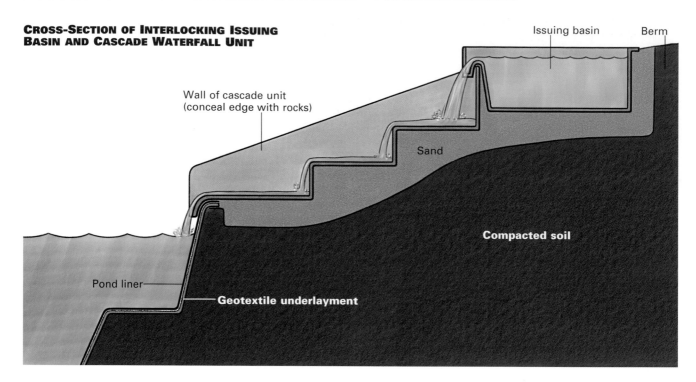

Issuing basin

Berm

Wall of cascade unit (conceal edge with rocks)

Sand

Compacted soil

Pond liner

Geotextile underlayment

Preformed waterfalls allow for simple do-it-yourself installation. Most preformed units are made of fiberglass or plastic; many look natural. Sizes range from a foot high to 6 feet or higher. You may choose from among units that include a built-in hidden filter. Use the manufacturer's guidelines for installation and its suggested range of gph to help you choose. Keep within the recommended gph, because too much flow can cause water loss and too little flow can result in a loss of visual and aural impact.

FIBERGLASS AND FOAM WATERFALLS

Experienced water gardeners recommend this type of small, preformed, portable waterfall installation for the first-timer. First, determine the appropriate size of submerged pump. Then select a site, such as a corner or patio garden, for the waterfall and place it there. Observe the setup for several days and decide whether to proceed with this site or try another one. Prepare the permanent site by making it level; tamp the ground to make it more stable.

Run tubing from the submerged pump to the connector piece of the waterfall. Use clamps to ensure a watertight connection at both ends. Adjust the position of the preformed waterfall to the exact spot you want, and plug the pump into the power line to commence operation. Camouflage the unit

with rocks and plants to help it blend with the surroundings.

POLYETHYLENE UNIT WITH BUILT-IN FILTER

Chose a waterfall that corresponds with your desired design. The filter capacity should match the size of your pond. Find out what capacity pump it takes to properly operate the waterfall/filter unit. Select a site adjacent to the pond where you plan to install the unit. Excavate the site as necessary to accommodate the unit. Tamp the soil firmly; cover the excavation with a 2-inch base of sand. Set the preformed unit in place. Make sure the unit overlaps the pond enough to help prevent water loss. Run tubing or flexible PVC pipe from the submersible pump to the unit, using clamps at both ends.

Attach the preformed waterfall to the flexible pond liner using screws and silicone sealant as detailed in the manufacturer's directions. Check to make sure the unit is level. Adjust the soil along the edge of the sand base to make it level. Install flat spillway rock for the water's return to the pond. Backfill around the unit using soil or sand. Integrate the surrounding spillway rocks with the surroundings using decorative rocks and plant material.

HIGH-DENSITY POLYETHYLENE AND FIBERGLASS CASCADE UNITS

Combine a series of cascade units that, when put together and overlapped, form a watercourse. Use brown or gray forms that match rocks indigenous to your area. Set each unit in its potential position. Change the configuration or placement as you wish. After you are satisfied with the layout, mark the perimeter of the units with stakes, sand, flour, or powdered limestone.

Excavate to support the units, allowing an additional 2 inches for a sand base. Tamp the sand and check that it is level, using a carpenter's level in all directions across the basin. If the basin is not level, water will be lost.

Place the lowest basin and cascade first. When installed, each unit's outside edges should rise 1 inch or more above the adjacent ground to protect the water feature from runoff. Backfill around the unit, using soil or sand, and check that the unit is level.

Temporarily connect tubing or pipe from the submerged pump to the top of the cascade unit. Make a test run of the unit, watching to ensure that the water in each unit stays at least 1 inch below the top edge of the unit. If not, empty the unit and adjust its placement accordingly. Repeat the installation for subsequent cascade units, making a water test following each installation.

Following the successful testing of the final cascade, install the permanent tubing or a pipeline alongside the watercourse, making

PLAN VIEW OF INTERLOCKING BASIN AND CASCADE WATERFALL UNIT

watertight connections at both ends. The line should maintain its original shape even when buried or walked on.

If the top cascade unit lacks a pipe fitting connection, run the water line over the top end of the cascade unit to discharge the water into the basin. Diffuse the flow of water by placing rocks at the point of discharge or by perforating the water line at the top of the cascade.

Camouflage the edges of your watercourse and help blend it with the surroundings by placing rocks and plants around its edge.

INSTALLATION OF PREFORMED BASIN AND CASCADE

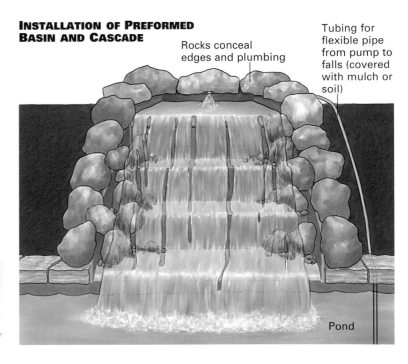

CUSTOM DESIGNS

Preformed waterfalls and cascade units come in a wide range of designs, but most retailers just stock a few models. Custom-order the design you want and allow extra time in your building plan for its manufacture and delivery.

CONSTRUCTING A NATURALISTIC WATERFALL

When it comes to installing large waterfalls, the job must be done right the first time. Fixing a bungled installation is time-consuming and costly. Contract a large-scale job such as this one to experienced professionals.

Your primary concern in constructing a natural-looking rock- and plant-lined waterfall will be to waterproof it. Most watercourses involve a flow of water between an upper basin, or header pool, and a lower, larger reservoir. It's possible to add a waterfall or watercourse to an existing pond.

Start by preparing an inclined site for the size and shape of the planned waterfall by berming or terracing it. The site should be gently sloping and wide enough to accommodate the waterfall as well as the surrounding rocks and plants. Carefully line and edge the watercourse to prevent water loss.

tamp the excavation. If the ground were to settle, the basin's edge and liner could become uneven and cause water loss. Make a ledge of earth around the perimeter of the excavation, elevated slightly to avoid water loss and to keep out unwanted surface runoff.

Cover the entire excavation with 2 inches of sand. Position a flexible pond liner over the excavation. This liner could be part of the main pond liner or a separate liner that overlaps it. If you use a separate piece, overlap it at least 12 inches over the main pond liner, and use a special adhesive tape made for liners (available from the liner supplier) to join the pieces.

MULTIPLE CASCADES

Multiple-cascade waterfalls (a series of waterfalls in a stream) should have a reservoir, or basin of water, to supply each cascade, starting with the smallest basin at the top and ending with the largest pool. Picture the watercourse as a staircase, its shape dictated by the site. A gently inclining watercourse will have long steps (the basins) with short risers; steep waterfalls will have shorter steps with tall risers. Vary the length and height of the steps to make the watercourse more natural-looking.

Make each basin level across its width; make the overflow area (spillway) 1 to 2 inches lower than the top edge. Thoroughly

ROCKWORK

If your plans call for heavy rockwork (rocks over 200 pounds), prepare for it before installing the liner. Determine the location of these large rocks, and set concrete slabs or poured-concrete footings to support their weight. Cover these foundations with geotextile or carpet remnants. Use at least two layers of scrap flexible liner between the heavy rocks and the liner. Place the liner over the area after the foundation sets.

Begin placing the rocks for the primary, or lowest, waterfall. Select and place each rock before you use mortar or black urethane foam to seal the rockwork and prevent water from going under or around the rocks. Then choose

Excavating the levels of your waterfall entails careful planning. Making certain the pools and spillways are level will help ensure their successful operation. The pools should be deep enough to hold water when the pump is turned off.

Placing boulders around the perimeter of the watercourse and putting a few here and there looks natural. Covering the bottom of the watercourse with gravel invites beneficial bacteria to colonize there enhancing the water quality.

A strong, flexible liner is relatively easy to install and helps prevent your watercourse from leaking. Use an underlayment to provide a soft padding for the liner and protect it from punctures.

Install a skimmer and a biofilter at opposite ends of a clear-water-type waterscape for a complete filtering system. Use an awl to poke holes in the liner; screw the skimmer to it.

At the top of the falls, the biofilter is installed in the ground, snugly surrounded by flexible liner and camouflaged with rocks. The biofilter tilts slightly forward to create the waterfall.

Finish the waterfall construction by using urethane foam and waterproof sealant to fill in between the rocks, holding them in place around the biofilter. Use the foam to secure spillway rocks as well.

CONSTRUCTING A NATURALISTIC WATERFALL
continued

**MULTIPLE-CATARACT
WATERFALL**

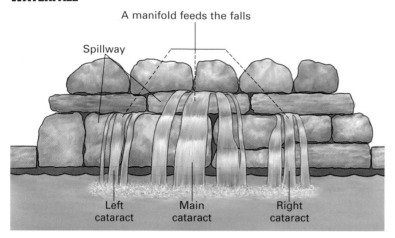

A manifold feeds the falls

Spillway

Left
cataract

Main
cataract

Right
cataract

**MAIN CATARACT OF
WATERFALL**

Gate or
ball valve

Issuing basin

Spillway

Berm

Sand

Sand

Liner

Geotextile underlayment

TEST THE FLOW

Before finalizing the configuration of rocks for a waterfall, test the water's flow over the spillway using a hose. See how the water flows and falls, and adjust the height and level of the rocks accordingly.

**LEFT AND RIGHT
CATARACTS OF WATERFALL**

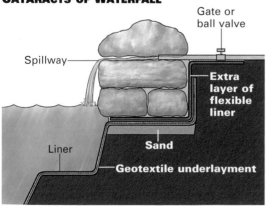

Gate or
ball valve

Spillway

Extra
layer of
flexible
liner

Liner

Sand

Geotextile underlayment

a large, flat rock for the spillway. Place this rock so it projects 2 to 3 inches beyond the rockwork below it. Use sealant as necessary to prevent water from going under or around the spillway rock. Repeat these steps as construction continues to the upper cascades. Arrange rocks around the edge of the falls and pools to conceal the liner and direct the water flow; the rocks flanking the falls should be higher than the spillway to help keep water in the channel.

Set rocks in mortar, if you prefer, although mortar doesn't survive freezing winters for long. For a better choice, spray expandable urethane foam into openings and crevices in the rockwork. Apply sealant discreetly to the back side of the rockwork; you don't want sealant to show on the front of the falls.

After finishing the liner and rockwork, install the piping, beginning at the bottom reservoir and working up alongside the watercourse to

the top falls. Allow at least two days for settling and curing before turning on the water to test the falls. Adjust the rock work to alter the water flow over the falls as necessary. Place small rocks in strategic spots to alter the flow patterns as desired.

MULTIPLE CATARACTS

Modify the construction somewhat if the waterfall design includes multiple cataracts or points where water emanates or discharges along the face of the falls. After installing the flexible liner, place rocks where you want them, but do not yet use any sealant. Study the rockwork to determine the desired water discharge points along the face. Next, disassemble the falls, carefully keeping track of which stones go where. Disassembly enables you to install pipes (rigid or flexible PVC), directed to each cataract. Construct piping to match the location of the water issue points. Use a ball valve for each discharge point. These valves must be accessible yet hidden from view. Reassemble the rockwork, sealing each layer with mortar or urethane foam.

When you finish installing the piping, connect it to the pump. Wait two days before turning water on to test the falls. Adjust the valve for each cataract to create the desired look across the face of the falls.

A FINISHING TOUCH

Use plants along the edges of the waterfall to conceal parts of the installation and give it a more natural appearance.

INSTALLING EDGING

Whether you choose some form of rock, wood, or plants for edging depends on the style and function of your water feature. Rock and stone are the most common and natural edging materials. Review the edging options described on pages 16 and 17, and consider the functional aspects of standing or sitting on edging to view, maintain, or otherwise access the water feature.

ROCK AND STONE

When edging a pond with a preformed liner or using heavy stonework on a flexible liner, build a masonry collar under the edge for adequate support. On a 2-inch layer of gravel, set a collar of concrete block or flat rock in a 1-inch layer of mortar. Extend the liner over the collar, then spread underlayment on top of it before setting the rock edging in place. Scatter smaller stones in between and behind the rocks to create a natural look. Set partially buried, larger rocks behind the edging here and there to complete the effect.

Place heavy edging rocks (weighing more than 150 pounds) on the ground around the perimeter of the water feature. Mortar or concrete isn't necessary as long as the rocks are situated in stable positions. Create a firm foundation for lighter-weight stonework edging by spreading a 3-inch layer of crushed rock. Top that with a 1-inch layer of concrete or mortar before setting the stones in place.

CONCRETE, MORTAR, AND pH

Mortar or concrete used for stabilizing edging is alkaline. As pond water and rain splash the material, lime is washed into the water feature and the pH of the water rises to levels dangerous or even fatal to fish. Neutralize the concrete or mortar by scrubbing it with a stiff brush and dilute vinegar as explained on page 71. Rinse the neutralized areas using water from a garden hose and pump the water out of the pond.

BRICK

Before laying a brick edge, make sure the perimeter of the water feature is level. A single layer of brick requires a 3-inch-thick foundation of crushed rock. Use paver bricks —the solid ones, not the ones with holes— as edging to minimize the invasion of weeds and grass among the edgers. Apply mortar under and between the bricks to make a sturdy edge.

WOOD

Set wood posts or logs vertically in concrete to form a pier-type edging. Use water-resistant wood planks or recycled-plastic "lumber" to build a deck or walkway along the water feature or jutting into it. Set the construction on concrete footings.

TURF AND PLANTS

Turf makes a neat edging, but it could get messy if soil washes out of the lawn into the water feature or grass clippings blow into the water when you mow. Prepare the edge for a lawn by excavating a shallow trench around the perimeter of the water feature and letting the liner extend into it. Cover the liner with a ledge of brick or flat rock set in mortar. Lay sod over the ledge to finish the edge.

Intersperse plantings with rocks and stones to create a natural-looking edge; avoid ringing the water feature with a single strand of rocks that looks like a necklace. Choose easy-care plants, such as low-growing evergreens, irises, and hostas. Ground covers and small beds of wildflowers also make excellent edgers. Choose plants suited to your climate as well as to your garden's conditions, including sunlight, soil, and moisture level. Stagger three, five, or seven plants around in clusters for effective results. Place tall plants on the far side of the water feature where they won't obstruct your view of it. Keep plantings simple: Too many different kinds of plants can create a busy, confusing scene.

Once the liner is filled, check for low spots around the top edge. If water is spilling out anywhere, lift the liner to fill in that spot with soil and gravel.

Leave at least 6 inches of liner showing around the edge of the water feature. To secure and hide the liner, carve a shallow trench, press the liner into it, and cover it with soil, rocks, gravel, and plants.

CONSTRUCTING A STREAM

Artistic, naturalistic rock placement makes the difference between a stream that looks contrived or one that appears created by nature.

Construct a stream much as you would make a waterfall, with a series of small, shallow pools and cascades along a gently sloping course. The longer the stream, the more likely it will meander as it follows the lay of the land. Construction methods depend on your choice of a liner.

sand base for the liner. Install the lowest component. In turn set each higher unit in place, fitting each unit to the adjoining ones by overlapping the top and bottom edges. The bottom overflow edge should be at the lowest point of each section. As you set each unit in place, check that it is level from side to side. After interconnecting all the stream units, test the water flow, using your garden hose or a temporary hookup from your pond pump to verify that the system works without losing water. If water escapes, adjust the units until they hold water without leaking.

Backfill the sides with sifted soil or sand and tamp thoroughly, being careful not to disturb the level position of the units. Hook up the pump and piping to test the water flow. Bury PVC pipe 2 inches deep alongside the waterway. Verify that the water level remains 1 to 2 inches below the top of the sides at all points. Adjust any unit as needed to meet this requirement.

Finish the stream by concealing the edges with rocks and plants. Place rocks in the streambed to create ripples and to form narrows that will speed the current. Cover the bottom of the liner with rinsed gravel to form a more natural-looking stream. Stones or gravel make cleaning the pond more difficult, but they provide extra surface area for beneficial bacteria to colonize in a stream.

PREFORMED STREAM UNITS

Installing preformed, high-density polyethylene or fiberglass stream units begins with creating a proper grade or smooth pitch down the course of the streambed. Create 2 inches of vertical drop for each 10 feet of horizontal run. Place the stream components in the desired orientation along the chosen route. Carefully mark the ground along the outside edges of the pieces, using small stakes, spray paint, or lime.

Remove the preformed units and excavate a trench for them so that the edge of each unit stands 1 to 2 inches above the adjacent ground, allowing for a 2-inch sand base under the forms. After excavating and tamping the ground, spread the

INSTALLING A FLEXIBLE LINER

Installing a flexible liner for a stream begins by creating an evenly pitched slope, as with a preformed unit stream. Mark the route of the stream with stakes or spray paint. Excavate the desired depth, allowing for a 2-inch sand base. Create a series of low cascades at various intervals, and make pools deep enough to retain water even when the pump is turned off.

Build up the outside border of the streambed with previously excavated soil. This helps to prevent runoff surface water from entering the stream. Create foundations or dams for the cascades within the streambed, using tamped soil, bricks, concrete blocks, or treated wood timbers under the liner. Cover these dams with geotextile underlayment or carpet.

THIN PLANTS

As marginal plants in the streambed mature and multiply, they may create a dam. Thin them periodically to prevent them from causing an overflow and water loss.

STREAM CONSTRUCTED OF PREFORMED UNITS

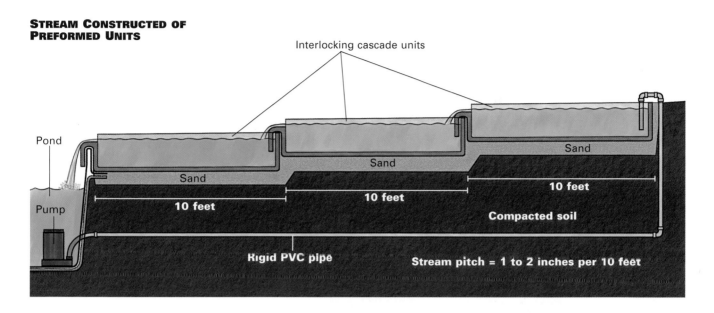

Interlocking cascade units

Pond

Pump

Sand

Sand

Sand

10 feet

10 feet

10 feet

Compacted soil

Rigid PVC pipe

Stream pitch = 1 to 2 inches per 10 feet

Ensure that the top of the streambed excavation is level across its width. As you check the level of the entire stream, adjust the sides as needed. Lay a 2-inch sand base on the bottom, add any foundation and underlayment, and install the flexible liner. Ideally, use a single piece for the entire length of the stream. If you use more than one piece, plan the connections for the cascade points, and lap the upstream liner section over the downstream liner section. Create a secure seam at each overlap point, using liner sealing tape.

PLACING ROCKWORK

First, set the rocks on the edges and the cascade points. Use a hose or a temporary hookup to the pump to mimic the water flow. Fill the stream and watch to make it stay within the lined area with no water loss. If you detect water loss, correct the situation by backfilling sand at the low points. Tamp the sand to prevent future compacting, which might cause another water loss.

When the stream proves itself watertight, place rocks in the flowing water to create ripples and velocity changes. Then check again for water loss. Cover the stream bottom with rounded, flat stones to conceal the liner. Check again for water loss.

Install piping along the streambed. Landscape around the stream to soften the rockwork and naturalize the area. Marginal plants and small independent bog gardens along the stream edge help to blend the stream with the surrounding landscape.

CLEAR OUT DEBRIS

Fallen leaves clog shallow, slow-moving streams in heavily wooded areas. To guard against water loss, include ample liner beyond the streambed to catch overflows and remove debris before it causes flooding.

This splendidly installed, natural-looking stream refreshes those who see and hear it. Especially on a hot summer day, it offers a cool oasis where you can get away for a little while.

INSTALLING PLUMBING

The complexity of plumbing depends on your choice of pump, the number of features it will operate, and the length of piping necessary to run them. Keep in mind a couple of guidelines as you plan to plumb your water feature: The stronger the pump, the greater the volume of recirculated water; longer vertical tubing or piping create greater resistance and reduce the volume of recirculated water.

PLEASE DON'T FEED THE PLANTS

Do not fertilize the plants in a plant filter. They're fed by the nutrient-rich water from the fishpond.

PUMP LOCATION

Placing the pump far from the waterfall promotes better distribution of the freshly oxygenated water by maximizing circulation across the pond. Locating the pump under a waterfall, however, offers greater efficiency by allowing it to recirculate more water with less effect than if placed away from the waterfall.

Set a submersible pump on clay bricks or another stationary platform to keep it a few inches above potentially pump-clogging debris that may accumulate on the bottom of the pond. Install a ball valve on the pump outlet, if you wish, to control the water flow. Use a diverter (three-way) valve to control two features operated by the same pump.

Use a bulkhead connector through the liner wall to provide a flooded intake for a nonsubmersible pump. If the pump is not self-priming and is located above the pond's water level, install a foot valve (check valve) and a strainer on the intake pipe. Make a housing for the pump to lessen its noise.

WATER LINES

Conceal and protect vinyl tubing with mulch or a thin layer of gravel. Rocks and foot traffic, for example, can collapse thin vinyl walls, restricting water flow. Generally use tubing with a diameter that fits the pump's discharge; choose tubing of the next larger size when running a line more than 10 feet horizontally.

Use flexible tubing or a hand-tight union connection to your pump. This allows easy access to the pump for servicing or removal. Clamp all other connections—especially any out-of-water ones—to be watertight.

Position the line that feeds an issuing basin at the head of a waterfall or stream to release its flow under the water surface. Within the basin, consider using perforated tubing with an end cap. The line can enter the basin between the edging and the liner. Camouflage it with rocks and plants.

MECHANICAL FILTER HOOKUP

Most mechanical filtration units work with water first passing through the filter, then

IN-AIR PUMP INSTALLATION

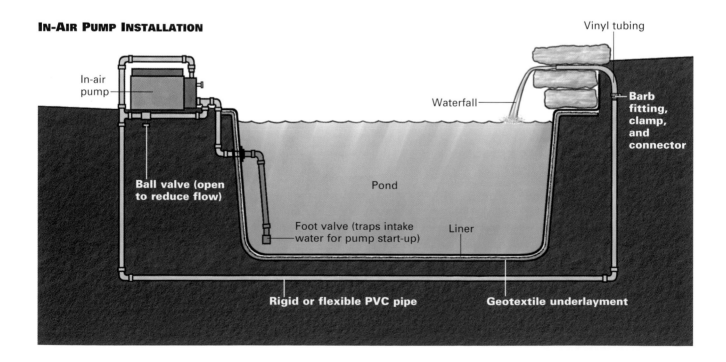

In-air pump

Vinyl tubing

Waterfall

Barb fitting, clamp, and connector

Ball valve (open to reduce flow)

Pond

Foot valve (traps intake water for pump start-up)

Liner

Rigid or flexible PVC pipe

Geotextile underlayment

passing through the pump. Make certain that the pump you choose for mechanical filtration has a threaded inlet so it is compatible with the filter unit. Find the pump's intake by removing the intake screen. Screw a threaded male hose barb fitting into the pump's intake. Install a short length of flexible vinyl tubing between the pump and the filter. Secure both ends of the tubing with clamps. Some mechanical filters come with a built-in pump assembled, saving you the task of assembly.

NONPRESSURIZED BIOFILTERS

Nearly all biological filters work outside of the pond without pressure. Because water discharged from one must flow by gravity, consider the site for it very carefully. Locate a nonpressurized biofilter where its discharge is higher than the water level of where the filtered water returns to the feature. Possible return points include under the edging of a pond, stream, or bog garden, or the top of a waterfall. Conceal the unit with a decorative wall, fence, or plant material to blend it into the landscape. Allow easy access to it for servicing.

Although a small biofilter can operate on solid ground, provide a concrete slab or poured footing to support the unit. Use a spirit level to confirm that you have a level base to help ensure the unit's stability. Connect flexible vinyl tubing or flexible PVC or rigid PVC pipe (as appropriate) for inflow and discharge lines. These conduct water from the pump into the biofilter and from the biofilter to the discharge point. Operate the pump to verify that the connections are watertight.

PRESSURIZED BIOFILTER HOOKUP

An advantage of a pressurized biofilter is that it can be located almost anywhere and be easily concealed. Set it in a garage, under

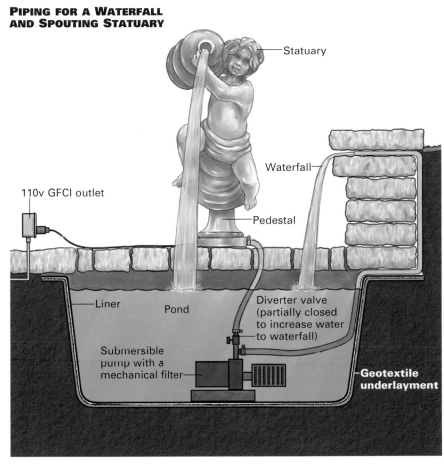

PIPING FOR A WATERFALL AND SPOUTING STATUARY

Statuary · Waterfall · Pedestal · 110v GFCI outlet · Liner · Pond · Diverter valve (partially closed to increase water to waterfall) · Submersible pump with a mechanical filter · Geotextile underlayment

With the right-size pump, you can run more than one water-moving feature, such as a waterfall and spouting statuary.

the deck, or in a buried vault. Smaller models operate with submersible pumps. These small pressurized units are often buried adjacent to the pond with only their top cap exposed for servicing. Larger pressurized filters utilize more powerful nonsubmersible pumps.

Connect the pond's bottom drain to the filter intake, and connect the filter outlet to a nonsubmersible, flooded-suction pump or self-priming pump. Pipe the pump's discharge to the filter's back-flush valve. Connect the discharge on the back-flush valve to a water line for release of the filtered water back to a waterfall, stream, or pond. Pipe the waste connection on the back-flush valve to a drain or any suitable discharge area for release of the nutrient-rich back-flush water. Start the pump and check the operation of the filter.

INSTALLING PLUMBING
continued

TYPICAL BIOFILTER INSTALLATION

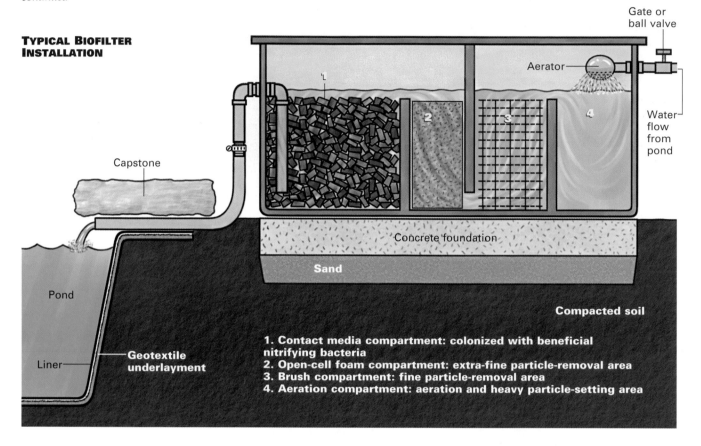

Gate or ball valve

Aerator

Water flow from pond

Capstone

Concrete foundation

Sand

Compacted soil

Pond

Liner

Geotextile underlayment

1. **Contact media compartment: colonized with beneficial nitrifying bacteria**
2. **Open-cell foam compartment: extra-fine particle-removal area**
3. **Brush compartment: fine particle-removal area**
4. **Aeration compartment: aeration and heavy particle-setting area**

KEEP CURRENT

Instructions given here apply to most filter units on the market when this was written. Be sure to consult the manufacturer's directions for the unit you purchase.

IN-GROUND FILTER HOOKUP

Excavate as required to accommodate a filter designed for in-ground installation. Make careful measurements to ensure that when you set the unit in the ground, its top is slightly above the pond's water level.

Install a level, tamped sand base, concrete slab, or poured concrete footing on which the filter can rest. Make the installation in tandem with the pond construction. Water will exit the pond through one or more bottom drains. A nonsubmersible pump at the end of the filter train sucks water through the filter system. The water level in the filter will match the pond's water level.

Filtered water travels from the filter through piping to the nonsubmersible pump. It draws water from the filter and forces it through piping to a waterfall, stream, bog garden, or pond. Install drain lines equipped with knife valves at the bottom of each filter chamber. In the case of multiple drain lines, combine them into a single line to direct drained filter water to a lower point or a sump pump. Create access from the ground surface to the buried knife valve handles with vertically aligned piping.

Recheck the level of the components and loosely backfill around the filter. Allow the filter to fill with water, then start the pump for a trial run. Make a final level check and pack down the backfill. Use previously described methods to conceal the filter (see page 79).

PLANT FILTER HOOKUP

Plan and install a plant filter as part of the pond construction project. Use a single piece of liner for the pond and the filter. Excavate an area adjacent to the pond 10 to 12 inches deep and equivalent to about 25 percent of the pond's surface area. Install a concrete block wall between the pond and the filter area, and level the top of the wall to be 2 inches above the projected pond water level. Install protection for the liner into the excavated area by covering the entire block wall with geotextile underlayment or carpeting. Install the liner into the pond, over the wall, and into the filter area. Use concrete to secure flat stepping-stones on top of the liner over the block wall, allowing 1- to 2-inch gaps between stones.

Construct a pipe manifold with 1½-inch rigid PVC pipe. Use one line with perpendicular branch lines connected every 2 feet or so. Cap the ends of the branch line. Make the manifold system to fit across the entire bottom of the filter area. Drill ⅜-inch holes approximately 6 inches apart at a 45-degree angle to the underside of the branch pipelines. Install the manifold in the bottom of the filter bed directly on the liner. Attach the manifold's main pipe to the pump discharge (located at the opposite end of the pond from the plant filter). Fill the 1-foot-deep filter area with ½-inch pea gravel. Place aquatic plants 18 inches apart; they will mature and fill in the filter after a year or two. Suitable plants include cattail, iris, pickerel rush, and arrowhead. Start the pump to initiate your new plant filter.

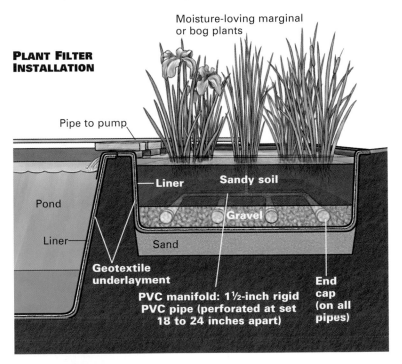

PLANT FILTER INSTALLATION

Moisture-loving marginal or bog plants

Pipe to pump

Liner

Pond

Liner

Sandy soil

Gravel

Sand

Geotextile underlayment

PVC manifold: 1½-inch rigid PVC pipe (perforated at set 18 to 24 inches apart)

End cap (on all pipes)

Using both a skimmer (above left) and a biological filter in a pond ensures crystal-clear water and enhances its quality. Unless the pond is properly stocked and balanced, you may need to check or clean the skimmer daily.

SEASONAL MAINTENANCE

SPRING MAINTENANCE

FISH

■ As water begins to warm and fish resume activity, begin to feed them minimally with a spring/fall high-carbohydrate food.

■ Inspect fish closely, looking especially for signs of parasites, sores, or lethargic behavior. If you have never added salt to your pond, add 1 pound of salt (solar, sea, or kosher; no iodine) per 100 gallons of water over a two- to four-day period. If you see symptoms of a fish disease or parasite, use a remedy formulated to eliminate it.

■ Test for ammonia and nitrite weekly. If levels are high, decrease feeding fish food until the biofilter takes effect and the ammonia and nitrite levels drop. If levels continue rising, use an ammonia-absorbing zeolite package in the waterfall-issuing basin or filter.

■ Add nitrifying bacteria to guard against potentially toxic buildup of ammonia from fish waste.

PLANTS

■ Clean up, weed, and mulch peripheral beds.

■ Return hardy aquatic plants to the pond if you removed them for the winter. Or, if you put them in the deepest part of the pond, relocate them for the growing season. Some water gardeners elevate hardy water lilies 3 to 4 inches below the water surface, where the warmer layer of surface water stimulates them to a faster start. After a water lily produces six pads, lower it to its normal growing range of 6 to 18 inches of water cover.

■ Add new marginal, submerged, and floating plants.

■ Divide root-bound plants and repot the divisions; give excess plants to friends or take them to a plant swap.

WATER FEATURE

■ Clean out debris that accumulated over winter.

■ Vacuum or sweep the pond bottom if there is a significant accumulation of leaves and other debris. Otherwise, drain the pond while removing its denizens, remove the accumulation, and rinse—don't wash—the pond before carefully restocking it, following the directions on page 90.

■ If a cloud of algae blooms, don't panic. This seasonal adjustment of the ecosystem is a natural occurrence.

■ Collect and add rainwater to top off the pond. Rainwater contains fewer chemicals than tap water.

EQUIPMENT

■ Reconnect the pump and filter, if stored over winter.

■ Check lights and electrical connections; make necessary repairs.

■ Inspect the liner and make repairs.

■ Start a biological filter by adding beneficial nitrifying bacteria. They're available in dry (less expensive) or liquid (faster-acting) forms from your water-garden dealer. A biological filter begins to function when the water temperature reaches the mid-50°s F.

■ Reinstall the UV clarifier with a new bulb.

Spring heralds renewed water-garden life. Plants bloom, fish spawn, and frogs croak.

SUMMER MAINTENANCE

FISH

■ As the water temperature rises above 60° F, switch from high-carbohydrate fish food to a high-protein product. If you have a light load of fish and plenty of beneficial nitrifying bacteria and submerged plants, you can feed your fish more. But if you have a full load of fish and few nitrifying bacteria and submerged plants, even this level of feeding could prove disastrous. These guidelines apply especially when a high fish population is combined with low oxygen levels and high summer temperatures.

■ Test the water weekly, checking the levels of pH, ammonia, and nitrite. If the pH rises above 8 or below 6.8, follow directions carefully when adding a pond remedy designed to change pH. Adjust pH in the needed direction by 0.1 point per day to reach the normal range of 6.8 to 8.0. If your fish have adapted to a pH of 8, you could postpone treatment unless and until the pH rises above 8.0. Check the pH at the same time daily.

■ Fish gasping at the surface of the water may indicate poor water quality (usually low oxygen content). However, it can indicate other problems, such as improper pH or some toxic matter. It may also suggest a gill problem. First, do what you can to increase oxygen. Keep the waterfall or fountain running 24 hours. Alleviate a moderate level of toxicity by removing one-third of the water. Replace it with water sprayed through the air from a garden hose (to release chlorine and absorb oxygen). If you use public water, add antichlorine or antichloramine treatment to the pond and replace no more than one-third of the pond's volume at a time.

■ Be vigilant about predators that visit your pond. Netting, electric fencing, scarecrows, imitation snakes and owls, and motion detectors connected to impulse sprinklers help deter predators. A watchful dog works most effectively.

THE POND

■ Be alert to any change in the rate of water flowing from a waterfall, fountain, statuary, or filter. This indicates an impediment, such as a clog in a pump intake or filter, kinked tubing, or a blocked water line. Keep water recirculating 24 hours a day through a biological filter. The more fish you have, and the hotter the weather, the more vital becomes recirculating water and increased oxygen in the water.

■ Summer evaporation accounts for the loss of up to an inch of water per week. If your pond consistently loses more than this, look for a leak. Begin by checking the waterfall or any other feature outside the pond walls, where about 90 percent of leaks appear. Otherwise, check the pond walls and bottom for leaks. Add water in the manner described above.

■ Control algae naturally using submerged plants and floating plants. Anacharis and cabomba, for example, along with water hyacinth and water lettuce, work by absorbing nutrients from the water so effectively that they starve algae to death. A properly sized ultraviolet clarifier turns green water clear within a day. Use a rake to remove filamentous algae.

Spend the summer relaxing near your water garden. It doesn't need weeding, hoeing, raking, or mowing.

PLANTS

■ Remove spent flowers, yellowing foliage, and excess plant growth.

■ Fertilize water lilies and other nonsubmerged aquatic plants with aquatic plant food. Follow the directions on the package.

■ Plant tropical water lilies and other tropical plants when the water temperature stays above 70° F.

■ Early in the season, divide overgrown water lilies and other aquatic plants that produce lots of leaves but few flowers. Lift the plants out of the water and split them into smaller plants. Repot and replace them in the water.

■ Introduce new plants to the water feature.

■ Remove weeds regularly.

■ Rake off overexuberant floating plants, especially if they cover more than 60 percent of the water's surface or cover the crowns of marginal plants.

■ If insect pests appear on plants, avoid using insecticides. Pick off pests or blast them off plants using cold water from the garden hose. Remove and dispose of thoroughly infested or diseased plants.

EQUIPMENT

■ Clean the pump intake weekly; clean the filter, skimmer, and light lenses regularly, as needed for efficient operation.

AUTUMN MAINTENANCE

Autumn brings a spectacular look, as well as many seasonal activities, to the water garden.

FISH

■ In cold climates, autumn marks the slowdown of fish and plant activity and the preparation for winter. When the water temperature drops below 60° F, switch from summer's high-protein fish food to the high-carbohydrate spring-autumn food. Cut back on feeding to every third day; gradually stop feeding fish until spring.

PLANTS

■ Remove floating and tropical plants when frost makes them unsightly.
■ Save tropical lilies in a greenhouse pool.
■ Move tropical marginal plants indoors and enjoy them as houseplants over winter.
■ As hardy water plants display frost damage, remove their foliage. Cut upright plant stalks 1 to 2 inches above the water surface (wait until spring to cut cattails and grasses). Cut submerged plants to within 6 inches of their containers. The greater volume of fish that reside in the pond, the greater the need to remove decaying (oxygen-consuming, sulfur dioxide-releasing) foliage.
■ Transfer hardy water lilies to deeper water where they won't freeze. Or remove foliage, wrap plants in moist newspaper, wrap loosely in plastic bags, and store in

a cool, dark area, such as a root cellar or an old, working refrigerator.

EQUIPMENT

■ Before leaves fall, install netting over the pond to prevent them from landing in the water and decaying. Support the netting with 2×4s or beach balls. Or purchase the type of tentlike netting structure that causes fallen leaves to slide down to the pond edges.
■ If you don't install netting, use a hand skimmer daily to remove leaves. Use a vacuum or leaf sweeper to remove leaves from the pond bottom. If you use a pond sweeper that's powered by a garden hose, add dechlorinator to the water before sweeping. If an inch or more of sediment has accumulated on the bottom, clean the pond before the weather makes it too cold to do the job.
■ When the water temperature drops into the 40°s F, remove, clean, and store your mechanical filter and pump, as well as the biofilter and pump. Install a thermostatically controlled floating pond heater in the final compartment of a large in-ground biofilter, if you have one, and change the water source from bottom drain to skimmer.
■ Drain pipes to prevent them from freezing and cracking. Turn off the water supply until spring.

WINTER MAINTENANCE

FISH

■ Discontinue feeding fish when the water temperature drops below 45° F. Resist the temptation to feed them during any midwinter warm spells. Cold quickly returns, making the fish too cold to digest food. The undigested food spoils in the fish's gut, a sometimes-fatal situation.

PLANTS

■ Leave the dead foliage of grasses and other perennials to stand at the edge of the water feature. This not only helps the plants survive winter, but it also offers an element of interest, as well as occasional protection for birds.

■ After the ground freezes, mulch around plants at the edge of a water feature. Spread a 4-inch layer of compost or shredded leaves on the ground to help preserve soil moisture and protect plants from the damage of winter's freezing-thawing cycle.

■ At least once a month, verify that your stored hardy water lily rootstock remains moist. Remoisten the newspapers if necessary.

■ Order new plants for spring arrival. Restock your water test kit and any other needed supplies at the same time.

EQUIPMENT

■ Remove the leaf netting to avoid snow buildup on it.

■ Try to prevent the pond from freezing solid if it contains fish and plants. Either remove the inhabitants and partially drain the feature or install a pond deicer.

■ Avoid smashing the ice; it can harm the fish.

■ Setting a pot of boiling water on the ice won't melt a hole and isn't advised.

■ Avoid operating the pump during freezing weather; it can damage the pump, the pipes, and the fish. Allow the pump to continue working only if you live in a mild climate where ice is a temporary occurrence.

■ Despite risks of freezing and damaging pipes, some waterfall owners keep their water feature running over winter. In cold climates, waterfalls should be shut down and the pump disconnected and stored until spring. A power outage in winter can ruin the works.

■ Protect a raised pond from ice damage by draining it to ground level.

In winter, your water feature can be just as attractive as in other seasons. In mild climates, the water remains ice-free throughout winter.

MAINTAINING YOUR WATER FEATURE

POND CLEANING

A water feature can function successfully for years without being cleaned. A full-fledged cleaning becomes necessary if the water feature accumulates an inch or more of sediment on the pond floor. Plan ahead in fall or spring so you can empty and refill the feature in one day.

Hose off the liner rather than scrubbing it so that beneficial bacteria and mosslike algae remain.

■ Prepare a temporary home for any fish and scavengers in a kiddie pool or a clean trash container in a shaded area, using water from the pond. Aerate the water with an air pump and air stones (preferred) or a recirculating pump that discharges water an inch or two below the water surface, making a gurgling rush of water rise several inches into the air.
■ Drain the pond until 6 inches of water remains. Be careful where you drain the pond. Flower beds and lawns relish the nutrient-enriched water; neighbors might not.

It's easier to net fish and scavengers at this point than trying to scoop them out of the water before draining the pond. Transfer them to their temporary home. Cover the container with netting to prevent the fish from jumping out.

■ Clean the filter while the water level drops.
■ Remove containers of plants from the pond. Cover the plants with wet newspapers and set them in the shade.
■ Continue draining the water feature until the pump cannot remove any more water. Use a plastic bucket to finish removing the water.
■ Collect debris and sludge from the bottom of the pond with a wet-dry vacuum or a broom and dustpan; do not use sharp metal tools.
■ Gently rinse the pond interior walls, allowing the mosslike algae and beneficial bacteria to remain clinging to the sides. Pump out the rinse water.
■ Make any necessary repairs to the water feature, especially if you have detected a leak.
■ Refill the pond, treating the water to remove chlorine and chloramine (if present). Also, treat the refilled pond with an anti-stress medication to benefit the fish.
■ Add an optional dose of salt (1 pound of solar or sea salt per 100 gallons of water) over two to four days to deter bacteria, fungus, and parasites.

If aquatic plants appear root-bound, divide them before returning them to the pond. In autumn, divide plants only if at least a month before anticipated frost remains.
■ Check the temperature and pH of the new water. Adjust the pH if it is more than 0.2 units different from the old water where the fish currently reside. Pump freshly treated pond water into the temporary fish home, slowly blending the new water with the old until the temperature difference is within 3°.
■ Net the fish and scavengers from the temporary home. Transfer them back to the pond in spacious buckets. Lower the buckets into the pond, then tilt them so the fish and scavengers can swim into their cleaned pond. It's OK to return water from the holding tank to the water feature; it contains beneficial microorganisms.

AUTUMN CLEANING

Fall ranks as the best time of year for cleaning the pond. Removing fallen leaves before they foul the water benefits fish all winter. Mild autumn temperatures and end-of-season robust health make it easier for the fish to withstand the stress associated with being handled.

REPAIRING A LEAK

LEAK DETECTION

If the water level in your feature drops more than 1 to 1½ inches per week, you have a leak. Waterfalls and streams account for leaks 9 out of 10 times. Shut off the waterfall or stream so that you can isolate a leak. Top off the pond. Wait 24 hours, then check the pond's water level. If you find that the pond remains full, you have confirmed that the leak is in the waterfall or stream.

If the pond loses water while the waterfall and stream are turned off, look for the leak by adding a trace of food coloring to the water. Sometimes, as a slow steady leak draws water, the dye makes it visible. Another method involves allowing the water level to drop until it stops. At that point, examine the liner's perimeter, marking the water level using a crayon or chalk on the liner.

Pump out another few inches of water if the reduced water pressure results in a slower leak. This also permits closer scrutiny of the suspected area. Monitor the dropping water level and remove pond inhabitants to temporary quarters before they suffer from insufficient water depth. The water level will sink to the bottom if that's where the leak exists. You might find the leak on the bottom even if the water drop stops a few inches above it. Regardless of whether a leak has formed on a sidewall or on the bottom, clean the area before examining it.

REPAIRING A FLEXIBLE POND LINER

Before making repairs, determine what caused a puncture, if possible. Remove any sharp objects under the liner and add fresh sand there, if necessary. Clean the area surrounding the leak with a plastic abrasive pad or steel wool (to promote a better bond between patching materials), and allow it to dry. Cut a patch of liner material remaining from the pond installation.

PUNCTURE REPAIR

Apply a thin coat of PVC glue (made for flexible, not rigid, PVC) to the patch for a PVC or PVC-E pond liner. Center the patch over the tear and apply uniform pressure over the patch with a wallpaper roller or a rolling pin. After 12 hours, refill the pond. For a punctured EPDM, butyl, or Xavan flexible liner, use a liner repair kit with adhesive-faced patches. If possible, insert a board behind the area being repaired. Remove the protective paper from the adhesive face and apply the patch over the hole. Apply uniform pressure over the face of the patch with a wallpaper roller, rolling pin, or burnishing tool. Refill the pond.

TEAR REPAIR

If a tear has caused a leak, apply two-sided liner sealing tape in a rectangular shape around the tear. Apply a patch of liner material the same rectangular size. Roll over the patch to secure it (as described above). Apply single-sided liner seaming tape over the edges of the patch. Refill your pond.

REPAIRING WATERFALL AND STREAM LEAKS

Settling under a waterfall or stream liner causes water loss as the water sprays outside of the area covered by the liner. In this case, disassemble the feature and rebuild it accordingly. Rodents might chew a hole in the liner, or maturing plants may cause water to rise higher than what the liner can control. Look for moist soil along the outside edge of the liner. Repair a puncture or tear in the liner as described above.

REPAIRING PREFORMED FIBERGLASS LINERS

Repair a crack or puncture in a fiberglass unit using a fiberglass repair kit. Look for the cause of the damage, and repair it to prevent a recurring leak. Roughen the area around the leak, using sandpaper. Apply a resin-soaked mesh patch according to the repair kit instructions. If your water-garden supplier doesn't stock the repair kits, check with a boat or auto supply store.

REPAIRING CONCRETE CRACKS

Temporarily remedy the cracks in concrete that appear over time as a result of settling, flaws in construction, or aggressive tree roots, by applying quick-setting concrete sealer. Apply the sealer to a clean, dry surface. If cracking is severe, line the entire pool with a flexible or preformed liner. Camouflage the edge of the liner as necessary. Alternatively, if faced with many hairline cracks, consider applying a liquid neoprene coating over the entire surface of the concrete.

CLEAN THE FALLS

To remove filamentous algae from a waterfall, shut off its water. Sprinkle the surfaces with solar or sea salt. The algae will die within 3 days. The waterfall washes the remains into the pond, and the filter removes them. The limited amount of salt doesn't harm plants or fish. (Fish and plants readily accept up to a pound of salt per 100 gallons of water.)

RESOURCES

You'll find a splendid variety of equipment, building supplies, and live goods at water garden specialists. The following retail suppliers sell by mail order, and most sell on the Internet too. Many suppliers also offer colorful, free catalogs with detailed information.

A Fleur D'eau
140 Route 202
Stanbridge-East
Quebec, Canada J0J 2H0
450-248-7008
fleurdo@netc.net

Green & Hagstrom
7767 Fernvale Road
P.O. Box 659
Fairview, TN 37062
615-799-0708
www.greenandhagstrom.com

Lilyblooms Aquatic Gardens
932 South Main Street
North Canton, OH 44720
330-499-6910
800-921-0005
www.lilyblooms.com

Lilypons Water Gardens
6800 Lilypons Road
P.O. Box 10
Buckeystown, MD 21717-0010
800-999-5459
www.lilypons.com

Lilypons Water Gardens
839 FM 1489
Brookshire, TX 77423-0188
800-999-5459

Maryland Aquatic Nurseries
3427 North Furnace Road
Jarrettsville, MD 21084
410-557-7615
www.marylandaquatic.com

Moore Water Gardens
(mail order)
4683 Sunset Road
P.O. Box 70
Port Stanley, Ontario N5L 1J4
Canada
519-782-4052
800-728-6324 Fax
Email: moorewg@execulink.com

Pacific Water Gardens
354 Pacific Street
San Luis Obispo, CA 93401
805-594-1693
www.pacificwatergardens.com

Patio Garden Ponds
2500 North Moore Avenue
Moore, OK 73160
800-487-5459
www.patio-garden-ponds.com

Slocum Water Gardens
1101 Cypress Gardens Boulevard
Winter Haven, FL 33884
863-293-7151
www.slocumwatergardens.com

Stewart's Garden Center
3253 Walker Road
Windsor, Ontario N8W 3R7
Canada
800-783-1470
www.stewartsflorists.com

Tilley's Nursery
111 East Fairmont Street
Coopersburg, PA 18036
610-282-4784
www.tnwaterworks.com

Tropical Pond & Garden
17888 61st Place North
Loxahatchee, FL 33470
561-791-8994
www.tropicalpond.com

The Water Garden
5594 Dayton Blvd.
Chattanooga, TN 37415
423-870-2838
www.watergarden.com

Water Garden Gems
3136 Bolton Road
Marion, TX 78124
800-682-6098
www.watergardengems.com

Waterford Gardens
74 East Allendale Road
Saddle River, NJ 07458
201-327-0721
www.waterford-gardens.com

Western Outdoor Aquatics
16150 Highway 7
Brighton, CO 80602
303-255-7081
888-277-3227
www.westernpond.com

COMMERCIAL SOURCES

MANUFACTURERS AND WHOLESALERS:

Aquascape Designs
www.aquascapedesigns.com

Beckett Corp.
5931 Campus Circle Drive
Irving, TX 75063-2606
888-232-5388
www.888beckett.com

Cal-Pump
13278 Ralston Avenue
Sylmar, CA 91342
800-225-1339
www.calpump.com

Charleston Aquatic Nurseries
3095 Canal Bridge Road
John's Island, SC 29455
800-566-3264
www.charlestonaquatic.com

Little Giant
P.O. Box 12010
Oklahoma City, OK 73157-2010
888-956-0000
www.littlegiant.com

Tetra Pond
3001 Commerce Street
Blacksburg, VA 24060-6671
800-526-0650
www.tetra-fish.com

United Pump
1772 Buerkle Circle
White Bear Lake, MN 55110
651-770-7810
www.unitedpumpinc.com

USDA PLANT HARDINESS ZONE MAP

This map of climate zones helps you select plants for your garden that will survive a typical winter in your region. The United States Department of Agriculture (USDA) developed the map, basing the zones on the lowest recorded temperatures across North America. Zone 1 is the coldest area and Zone 11 is the warmest.

Plants are classified by the coldest temperature and zone they can endure. For example, plants hardy to Zone 6 survive

where winter temperatures drop to –10° F. Those hardy to Zone 8 die long before it's that cold. These plants may grow in colder regions but must be replaced each year. Plants rated for a range of hardiness zones can usually survive winter in the coldest region as well as tolerate the summer heat of the warmest one.

To find your hardiness zone, note the approximate location of your community on the map, then match the color band marking that area to the key.

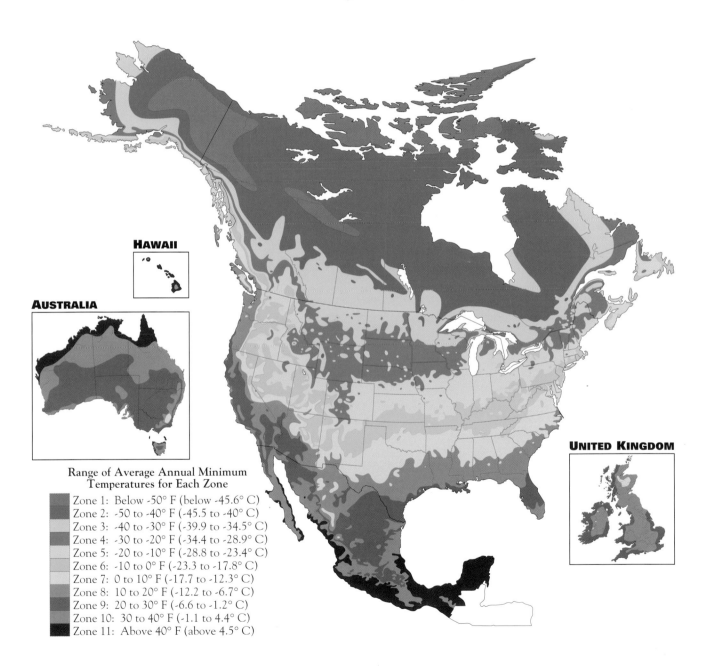

Range of Average Annual Minimum Temperatures for Each Zone

Zone 1: Below -50° F (below -45.6° C)
Zone 2: -50 to -40° F (-45.5 to -40° C)
Zone 3: -40 to -30° F (-39.9 to -34.5° C)
Zone 4: -30 to -20° F (-34.4 to -28.9° C)
Zone 5: -20 to -10° F (-28.8 to -23.4° C)
Zone 6: -10 to 0° F (-23.3 to -17.8° C)
Zone 7: 0 to 10° F (-17.7 to -12.3° C)
Zone 8: 10 to 20° F (-12.2 to -6.7° C)
Zone 9: 20 to 30° F (-6.6 to -1.2° C)
Zone 10: 30 to 40° F (-1.1 to 4.4° C)
Zone 11: Above 40° F (above 4.5° C)

INDEX

Page numbers in bold denote figures or photographs.

METRIC CONVERSIONS

U.S. Units to Metric Equivalents			Metric Units to U.S. Equivalents		
To Convert From	Multiply By	To Get	To Convert From	Multiply By	To Get
Inches	25.4	Millimeters	Millimeters	0.0394	Inches
Inches	2.54	Centimeters	Centimeters	0.3937	Inches
Feet	30.48	Centimeters	Centimeters	0.0328	Feet
Feet	0.3048	Meters	Meters	3.2808	Feet
Yards	0.9144	Meters	Meters	1.0936	Yards
Square inches	6.4516	Square centimeters	Square centimeters	0.1550	Square inches
Square feet	0.0929	Square meters	Square meters	10.764	Square feet
Square yards	0.8361	Square meters	Square meters	1.1960	Square yards
Acres	0.4047	Hectares	Hectares	2.4711	Acres
Cubic inches	16.387	Cubic centimeters	Cubic centimeters	0.0610	Cubic inches
Cubic feet	0.0283	Cubic meters	Cubic meters	35.315	Cubic feet
Cubic feet	28.316	Liters	Liters	0.0353	Cubic feet
Cubic yards	0.7646	Cubic meters	Cubic meters	1.308	Cubic yards
Cubic yards	764.55	Liters	Liters	0.0013	Cubic yards

To convert from degrees Fahrenheit (F) to degrees Celsius (C), first subtract 32, then multiply by ⅝.

To convert from degrees Celsius to degrees Fahrenheit, multiply by ⅖, then add 32.